ENDORSEMENTS

"*Happywork* is an avant-garde fable about all the absolutely worst companies you could ever imagine rolled into one. Believe me, if you have an issue with your workplace—and here it is. As you may have guessed from the title, this is an upbeat book. Chris Reimer does a fabulous job of laying out the principles for making work a decent—nay, a great—place to be."

—Daniel H. Pink, author of *To Sell is Human* and *Drive*

"In this wisdom-filled, compelling story, we learn why team members who genuinely and authentically feel good about themselves, their work, and their contribution make not only for an inspiring workplace, but results in a significant increase in a company's bottom line. Every leader—and those who desire to be effective leaders—should own this book, devour its contents, and keep it as a resource. You'll want to make sure you have access to 'Charlie' for those times you need a trusted mentor to remind you of these valuable lessons."

—Bob Burg, co-author of *The Go-Giver*

"At the end of the day, if you're not happy with what you're doing for a living, you won't love it, and when you don't love what you do, you can't do it to the best of your ability. Read this book, and learn to work happy."

—Peter Shankman, author of *Zombie Loyalists*, and all-around happy guy

"Commitments are at the heart of *Happywork,* and I'm fully behind Chris Reimer's concept. I wish more businesses were this happy."

—CHRIS BROGAN, CEO Owner Media Group and New York Times bestselling author of *The Freaks Shall Inherit The Earth*

"The values of the business world are slowly changing, but they need to change more quickly. In my experience, a more satisfying life should be priority #1. Read this book and make the change you want to see."

—JOHN JANTSCH, author of *Duct Tape Marketing* and *Duct Tape Selling*

"In his engaging story, Chris shows us what's wrong with the corporate world. And how to fix it."

—DAVID MEERMAN SCOTT, bestselling author of *The New Rules of Marketing and PR*, now in over 25 languages from Bulgarian to Vietnamese

"Storytelling is the basis for great marketing and connection. Chris employs it here to great effect, helping us to understand the 'why' and 'how' of changing a business culture to create an environment that leads to happiness and success."

—TED RUBIN, bestselling author of *Return on Relationship*

"The brilliance of *Happywork* is the clarity it brings to business challenge #1—finding fulfillment at work."

—DAVE GRAY, founder of XPLANE, and author of *The Connected Company*

"An entertaining book that will leave you inspired and ready to create a work environment that people will thrive in."

—JOHN MICHAEL MORGAN, author of
Brand Against The Machine

"A parable of hope, a parable of joy."

—MARK SCHAEFER, author of *Return on Influence*

"*Happywork* will resonate with everyone from CEOs to Human Resources to anyone who has ever worked in a cubicle or an office. More importantly, perhaps, because most of us have, at one time or another, worked in at least one company where we've felt maligned and mistreated, this book will confirm that you were right all along about how work life should be. And for the 'higher ups,' this book will show you exactly how a better work life makes for a better bottom line."

—SUSAN BARONCINI-MOE, executive coach, digital marketing strategist, and author of *Business in Blue Jeans*

"*Happywork* is a shockingly realistic look at the common workplace and a blunt reminder that employment misery is unacceptable. Life is too short! It's time for a change, and this book will get you started."

—JASON SURFRAPP, author of *Creativity for Sale*

"Remember Harvey Keitel's character in *Pulp Fiction*? He played "The Wolf"—he was the guy they brought in to clean up the mess. Sam Maslow is that guy in *Happywork*. Dick Vunorri has hired the ideal person to transform his company. The journey Reimer takes us on is cringe-worthy, suspenseful, entertaining, and educational. A wonderful read!"

—DAVE DELANEY, author of *New Business Networking: How To Effectively Grow Your Business Network Using Online and Offline Methods*

"*Happywork* shows you how to create significance both personally and professionally. Get more pleasure out of your life and greater fulfillment at work."

—SAM SILVERSTEIN, author of *No More Excuses*

"*Happywork* is Chris Reimer's cry from the heart for humanizing the workplace. Reimer dramatizes essential practices for creating both workplace satisfaction and business success. If you care about talent retention, employee engagement, and how to create a thriving, happy organization, read this book!"

—STEVE KNIGHT, Director, COCAbiz

"The average human will spend a lifetime working. Why can't we make that time great? *Happywork* is the blueprint for a new business culture. Chris Reimer shows us the fallacy of a business determining success based solely on numbers and offers an alternative—a happy one"

—ZEB WELBORN, owner of Welborn Media, Host of the *Defining Success Podcast*

"My goodness, honey. This is incredible. I can't believe you did this."

—MY WIFE, and probably my biggest supporter

HAPPYWORK

A BUSINESS PARABLE ABOUT THE JOURNEY
TO TEAMWORK, PROFIT, AND PURPOSE

CHRIS REIMER

Sound Wisdom

P.O. Box 310

Shippensburg, PA 17257-0310

For more information on foreign distribution, call 717-530-2122.

Reach us on the Internet: www.soundwisdom.com.

Cover Design by: Steve Hartman

Author Photo by: Bill Sawalich

ISBN 13 TP: 978-0-7684-0531-6

ISBN 13 Ebook: 978-0-7684-0532-3

For Worldwide Distribution, Printed in the U.S.A.

1 2 3 4 5 6 7 8 / 19 18 17 16 15

DEDICATION

To my wife, Julie, and my daughters, Clara and Ella.

And to you, the despondent, struggling soul, fighting a personal battle we know nothing about. Hang in there.

CONTENTS

PART ONE

RESPECT FOR THE WORK PROCESS

"What we have to learn to do, we learn by doing."
—ARISTOTLE

"I like work. It fascinates me. I can
sit and look at it for hours."
—JEROME K. JEROME

"Opportunity is missed by most people because
it is dressed in overalls and looks like work."
—THOMAS EDISON

"If you had to identify, in one word, the
reason why the human race has not achieved,
and never will achieve, its full potential,
that word would be 'meetings.'"
—DAVE BARRY

CHAPTER 1

A CLEANUP JOB

"You have 30 days, Mr. Vunorri."

"*What*???" Dick shouted into his office phone.

"This bank is not a charity, and we don't look too kindly on four overdue interest payments, a tapped-out line of credit, and unreturned phone calls."

"But we've been your loyal customer for years!"

"And we appreciate your business, but..."

"You keep switching bankers on me! It's impossible to establish a working relationship with you. Look, you gotta give me more time!"

"We've given you more than enough time. In deference to the long relationship we've had with your father, we've shown extreme patience."

"Guys, I need more time."

"This *is* more time. You have 30 days to provide us a working plan—one that we approve—on how you're going to right the ship. Vunorri needs to begin paying down this line of credit, and we need a payment schedule for the overdue interest payments. We don't want to liquidate your business. However, unless you can come up with this money, you'll leave us no choice. A plan, 30 days from today, or we'll have to start foreclosure proceedings."

Dick fumbled the phone as he grabbed a pen and his calendar. "OK," he sighed. "I'll hit the deadline. I have a guy I can call. A turn-around specialist..."

When the call came in on Sam's cellphone, he didn't recognize the number. He had a strict policy of never answering "stranger" phone calls, which, out of a peculiar mixture of adventure and addiction, he broke constantly. Of course, it made financial sense to answer those calls. A consultant never knows where the next job is going to come from.

"This is Sam Maslow."

"Hi Sam, my name is Dick Vunorri. Jerry Singleton at Abacus referred me to you. He's a good friend of mine. He told me you did some great work for his company."

"Indeed," Sam said. "We made some big changes at Abacus. They're in much better shape now. What can I do for you?"

"I'm the president of Vunorri Inc. We manufacture electronic components and distribute them domestically and internationally. We're facing some major financial and operational challenges, and I understand that's your specialty. I'm wondering if you can assist us."

"I may be able to help," Sam said. "Would you like to meet and discuss?"

"Absolutely," Dick answered. And he lobbed that answer over the net quickly. "Are you available for hire immediately?"

"I do have capacity right now."

"Perfect! Can you come by at two o'clock today?"

After a nearly 20-year career as a CPA, Sam had grown bored. Performing and managing hundreds of audits had taught him a great deal about business and the numbers, but he wanted to do more. Instead of merely depicting and verifying a company's financials, he wanted to change them for the better. Turning companies around afforded him the chance to really move the needle, and giving businesses what they needed most, when they needed it most, also allowed him to increase his earning power and set his own schedule.

He deeply appreciated entrepreneurs and the businesses they built, and was now a one-man entrepreneurial show himself. He relished the role of the "fix-it guy" who comes in and solves the problem a company couldn't solve themselves. He may have even once deluded himself into thinking of his role as the "mercenary" or "hired gun." He *was* good. Companies, both local and national, called him when they needed help. His advice was not always easy to hear—"You need to cut staff," "This person has to go," "Restructure this department," "Stop selling this product," "Close these underperforming locations." Sam was a master at compartmentalizing people, streamlining processes, and creating systems of control. Black is black and white is white, and Sam reliably found and implemented solutions on those peripheries. The numbers never lied, and there was comfort to be found in them. If the financials could be coaxed into the black, he was in the win column.

The recommendations he made to clients often left collateral damage, even a wake of destruction depending on the severity of the crisis faced. He didn't devote time to worrying about this; saving companies was his gift to the people who paid his fee and the employees who remained employed after he was gone. Life wasn't fair, and it didn't have to be. To make things work, sometimes bad things had to happen to good people. If business tasted like vanilla, nothing would ever get invented. Amazing businesses would never get started; empires would go unborn.

And, hey, the money was good. You don't need to know what kind of car Sam drove, except to say it was nicer than yours. The hours were long, but that didn't matter to him. "Workaholic" is such a negative word. Sam was an executioner, someone who always finished the job. No matter the scene, he'd outwork and outsmart his opponent. Failure was a foreign concept to him. Some hard-nosed businesspeople made it personal—me vs. you—but not Sam. He didn't need to gin himself up to push through and win. It was simply about victory in business, because *why not?* For Sam, the object of his affection was the work, and himself. While his absence from the home might have mattered to his wife and daughter, it was a nondiscussion, a moot point. Sam worked, Sam achieved, and Sam won.

"Nice to meet you, Sam! Right this way." Dick led Sam off the elevator onto a quiet fourth floor with several nicely appointed offices and a wood-paneled conference room. Dick was a tall, fit man and looked to be in his mid-50s. He was lean, with broad shoulders and big hands. He still had a youthful face, with a square jaw and blue eyes. His short salt-and-pepper hair was perfectly cut, and he had a penchant for wearing nice clothing. So he looked like a company president. He was gregarious, excitable, and prone to smile, which was curious, considering his predicament.

"Well, as I'm sure Jerry told you," Sam said, "I'm a turnaround specialist based here in town. I help organizations solve their problems.

Business challenges take many forms, and I can help in many ways. I have experience with financial statements, cost accounting, human resources, marketing, and especially operational architecture—are people 'sitting in the right seats on the bus?' I come in and assess the situation, leaving no stone unturned."

Dick blurted out, "That sounds *great*. When can you start?"

This immediately raised Sam's antenna. Even with his sterling reputation, people at his hourly rate were rarely hired without at least a brief discussion. Was Dick just not that sharp, or were things much worse than Sam even imagined? Or was this Dick's idea of a "brief discussion?"

"First, Dick, I need to hear what your challenges are to make sure I can help you guys," Sam said. "While I'm *very good* at what I do, Jerry's recommendation aside, you should probably size me up as well."

"I trust Jerry's judgment," Dick shot back.

"Well...Jerry *is* a smart fella," Sam responded. "You don't even know how much I cost yet."

"Money won't be an issue," Dick said.

"Look, let me be up front with you. I'm the kind of consultant who'll tell you how it is. It's nothing personal. I take my job very seriously. It's the principle of the thing. If I have an idea that can help you, it's my duty to share it with you, even if it's not something you're going to want to hear. My methods aren't always popular with people, but the problems I'm dealing with are usually pressing. If you have too many employees, or unprofitable locations, you're going to get recommendations from me that'll have your HR department very busy.

"All of this sometimes rubs people the wrong way, but..."

"No problem at all," Dick interjected. "If we retain you, I want you to shoot me straight. Deal?"

"Yes, that *is* how it has to be. To start, why don't you tell me a bit about your organization."

Dick laid out Vunorri's history, explaining that his father founded the company back in 1969 with a $5,000 investment. He hired his first employee less than a year later, and built a nice little team. They experienced growth over the years, expanding the warehouse and manufacturing area twice. Dick joined the company in his late 20s, and had been working there for almost 25 years. He finally took over the role of president from his father seven years previously.

"We're facing challenges from every direction," Dick explained. "China, squeezed margins, young employees who aren't as loyal as their predecessors, you name it. Our turnover is just...we keep losing good people, Sam. I don't understand it. We pay people well, but attitudes are terrible."

"What do you think is causing this?" Sam asked.

"I just don't know," Dick answered. "I think that's why you're here. I...I don't even know where to begin. You're one of the few people I've ever even admitted this to. It's not easy being a leader who doesn't know what to do next. I have an MBA, a ton of experience here at the company. It just feels like it's..." Dick paused, his face contorting with a mixture of thought and a little pain. In a quavering voice, he continued, "It feels like it's all kind of slipping away. Am I making sense?"

Sam established firm eye contact with Dick, with the hope of reassuring him. "Yes, I know how you feel. I've never run a company this large before, but I do know how hard it is. You're not the first stressed-out CEO I've sat across from. Let me ask you this: Is the product...do you make a high-quality product?"

"You bet we do," Dick said enthusiastically. "We can compete on quality with most anyone."

"You're not receiving excessive customer complaints, poor Better Business Bureau ratings, losing big clients, anything like that?"

"No, no, not at all. I would know about that if it were happening. Our problem is cash flow. Well, it's more than that." Dick stopped talking for a moment to collect himself.

"Reserves are dwindling, and our line of credit at the bank is maxed out. My CFO and his team are juggling the bills as best they can. My bankers want answers, and I don't know what to tell them. They just gave me an ultimatum—they're going to start foreclosure proceedings in 30 days unless I provide them a plan to get us out of this mess." Sam now understood why Dick wanted to bring him on immediately.

"I haven't told our employees this," Dick said, "and I hate even admitting it to you. It feels like the walls are closing in. We're a failing business, and you're my last-ditch effort to figure out why."

Sam gave some thought as to what might be causing the trouble. He knew people always wanted quick answers, and Dick certainly needed answers yesterday. But Sam was not a quick-answers kind of guy. He understood how complicated running a business was, and judging by his discussion with Dick, there were probably all sorts of things wrong with Vunorri Inc. He was interested in the assignment and wanted to close on the proposal.

"Dick, I can help you. I can't tell you what's wrong without really diving into your business, and I hope you understand that."

"Yeah, sure, what do you have in mind?"

"Well, you should embed me in the company for four weeks. You can let the bank know I'm here—they know me. I need to tear this place down to the studs to truly understand it. I need access to information—financials, employee records, everything. I need to interview everyone who works here."

"Holy cow," Dick exclaimed with a hand on his forehead.

"Being thorough is going to give us the best chance to identify what's wrong and impress the bank. Can we make it happen?" Sam asked.

"Wow," Dick said. He thought about it for a moment. "Yes, I can tell people to cooperate."

"Sure, you could do that. I guess what I'm asking is...can you roll this out in a way that'll get your people really opening up to me?"

"I think so."

"I don't want to waste your time," Sam said. "To get a plan to the bank that they'll buy off on, I'm really going to need access and cooperation. Can this work?"

"I'm not going to tell everyone about the foreclosure stuff, but I can pull together our managers and staff and explain what we're doing. Maybe you can be there to introduce yourself and answer any questions."

After the slightly unpleasant exchange where they discussed compensation for a four-week engagement, it was settled. Sam would be back tomorrow. He had every confidence in the world that he'd be able to produce results at Vunorri. As long as the company hadn't slipped beyond saving, he knew he could help them. If there was fat to trim, he'd find it. He'd been on this bicycle before.

Actually, Sam had no idea what was about to befall him.

CHAPTER 2

THE CRAZY UNCLE

Just the day before, Sam was in between consulting jobs. Fourteen hours later, on a cloudless, crisp Tuesday morning, he arrived back at Vunorri for day one of his assignment. He was eager to dive in and would begin with Dick Vunorri. Sam usually started such turnaround assignments by interviewing the president or CEO. Organizational leaders always divulged the best intelligence and gave great clues on which departments needed the most attention.

"Good to see you, Sam," Dick said. "I've set up your office here, on the first floor, close to the action. If you ever need anything, come find me. Are you ready to get started?"

"Yes. Let's have a seat and talk about your finances. Tell me what's going on."

"Margins are down. My CFO, Neil, will provide you some reporting. We're having a hard time competing with the Chinese. Our product is higher quality, and there are some consumers willing to pay for it. But for us, competing on price is difficult. Here's what I don't get: our job costing models look good. Our margins should be better." He went on to provide some more details, with Sam dutifully taking notes. Dick then talked about employee morale. In the seven years he had been CEO, turnover had risen over 50%, and all of this put together really had employees' stomachs in knots, including Dick's himself.

"Frankly, Sam, this place isn't like it used to be. I haven't taken a raise in two years. We should be making more money. I didn't even bonus myself last year. It's taking a financial toll on my family. If the bank forecloses, I'll have to downsize. We won't be able to maintain our lifestyle, and my wife won't let me hear the end of it. Our marriage isn't what it used to be, either. And because of all of *that,* I can't stop thinking about work. I don't sleep well at night. And my dad..."

Dick's dad had a knack. The patriarch of the Vunorri family, he had a way with people. He always knew what to do, what to say. Now retired, his wisdom came in quick, intermittent spurts, if it came at all. He labored for years to groom Dick to be the leader of Vunorri, and like most company founders, he had trouble letting go. Dick was not the carbon copy visionary he had intended to hand his company to, but once Dick became President, he took his hands off the wheel and let his son run the show. Finding it necessary to engage an expensive turnaround specialist at this late hour suggested that the transition of power yielded mixed results.

"Dad came from humble beginnings. He didn't have an MBA or parents made of money. He just worked harder than everyone else. And the world was simpler then."

"What do you mean?" Sam asked.

"Challenges today are huge. The rise of Chinese manufacturing, skyrocketing health insurance costs, people saying whatever they want about you on social media, bankers who won't leave you alone! Sam, our workforce is less loyal than years ago. We train people to become great, and less than a year in, they just leave! And customers' budgets aren't what they used to be. We used to get huge sales with not much effort. Now we have to compete for every dime. It's just tough."

After pausing for a moment, he took a deep breath and laid it out. "Sam, I really want to get this place humming again. I don't want to let my dad down, don't want to squander the decades of work he put into this place. Now *my* son works here. I want to hand a healthy company to him someday. But this bank ultimatum...I don't want them to take my company."

Then, a jarring moment. Dick leaned in, closer to Sam, grabbed his forearm with gusto, and said, "Please help us." Thankfully, Sam was not a "You're violating my personal zone!" kind of guy.

"Dick, that's why I'm here. I still don't know what I still don't know, but that's the very reason I've recommended this thorough study. I'm going to..."

"Sam," interrupted Dick, "I want you to come in, and I want you to shake things up!"

With experience come guideposts that one has previously passed, phrases one has heard before. Sam had heard this before. Many a CEO would bring Sam in because it meant *action*! But what they really wanted was the *appearance* of action, the simulation of forward motion. They wanted to convince themselves they were attacking the problem. Or maybe they thought they wanted action, but change was too painful for them to endure. For Sam, "Shake things up!" was often code for "nothing is going to change." Mere bombast. He usually waded through such waters with the numbers—they always made for a convincing argument. Sam would figure out where the problem was and write a turnaround plan to please the bank. If Vunorri Inc. didn't follow his advice, that was on them.

"Get the bank off my back, Sam. I need that plan. Clean house! Who should we get rid of? This is your directive."

"No problem, Dick. I'm on it." Perfect. As if conducting international affairs, the "nuclear option" was not off the table. Music to Sam's ears.

It was time for lunch. Sam loved dining out, but when on a consulting job, he tried to stick around and observe employees. If his client had a lunchroom or a cafeteria, he liked to grab a bite there and take a temperature of the mood. He'd strike up conversations and gain confidences, trying to get intel. Some of his most impressive strategies had been culled from such encounters. Employees would sometimes spill the beans to Sam out of frustration. They had been trying to get their bosses to listen for so long, with little success, and along came Sam to lend an ear.

Vunorri had a lunchroom with some vending machine sandwiches, so he availed himself of a Monte Cristo (Maybe he *would* go out tomorrow!). He approached a table.

"Mind if I join you?" Sam asked.

"Not at all. Have a seat, my friend."

"My name's Sam."

"I'm Charlie. I work in the mailroom."

"Nice to meet you, Charlie. This is my second day on-site—first day I've had the chance to sample this fine processed food." Charlie let out a not-so-loud belly laugh.

"It ain't so bad, once your body acclimates," Charlie said.

Charlie had a wise voice, with a radio-like tenor and a confident cadence. Sam pegged him at around 75 years of age. His grey hair was combed to the side and slightly disheveled—he wore it well. This day, he was sporting a short-sleeve dress shirt, which offended Sam's fashion sensibilities. Such foibles could be forgiven.

"I've been retained by Mr. Vunorri to study the company's operations and make recommendations," Sam said.

"Oh I know who ya are. Dick pulled the entire company into the warehouse yesterday afternoon and let us in on your arrival."

"What the hell…?" Sam thought. He was supposed to be in that meeting to introduce himself.

"Welcome. How long are you gonna be here?"

"I told Mr. Vunorri it would be four weeks. I'm never sure how long my work will take, but clients don't like things to be open-ended."

"Afraid you'll suck 'em dry, huh?" Charlie asked.

"I suppose. A great reputation and all the references in the world won't change that mindset."

"Well, my friend," Charlie said, "welcome to our little company. You're in for a heck of a ride."

"Why do you say that?"

"Well, I don't know how much I should say. I mean…you got hired for a reason, right? This place needs help."

"What kind of help?" Sam asked.

"I think you'll figure it out as you go," Charlie said. "Lemme say this: if you're good…if you poke and prod…if you ask 'why' a lot… you'll amass a whole boatload of advice to give to Dick. The question is, what kind of advice does he want you to give him?"

"What do you mean?" Sam asked. "I'll assess the situation here and give him my *best* advice."

"Sam, I think we both know perfectly well what I mean. I've seen *Office Space*. You're the consultant! I know your methods. We know your role. Who stays? Who goes?"

"Hold on a minute, sir..."

"You call me Charlie now, ya hear? Listen, it is what it is. We're in financial trouble. Dick needs to know what to do next. You're going to go to your toolbox and do what you do best, right?"

"Toolbox?" Sam asked.

"We're hurting, and you're here to fix it, at any cost. And more often than not, you recommend layoffs, right?"

"Who *is* this guy?" Sam thought to himself.

"Look, I've probably said enough," Sam said. "It was nice to meet you."

"Well bud, I wish you luck during your four weeks here," Charlie said. "Just know this: layoffs aren't always the answer. No one here wants to lose their job. Hopefully you can save the day."

"Thanks for the vote of confidence," Sam said. "And thank you for the suspiciously grudging introduction to Vunorri. You know, as part of my process, I plan on interviewing you."

"I look forward to it," Charlie responded dryly. "How come you'd interview someone like me?"

"It's like you said. Ask 'why' a lot and see what shakes out. The answers are within these walls somewhere. It's not always about getting rid of people, you know."

"Even though it often is, right, Sam? Listen, I need to get back to work. Good luck. Maybe I'll see you here tomorrow."

It can be said with confidence that Charlie was the prickliest mailroom employee Sam had ever encountered. It was Sam's job to have uncomfortable conversations, but that was ridiculous. Spanning his entire career, from junior auditor to highly-paid consultant, no one had ever had the nerve to cross him like that.

Still, Charlie was right: Sam had helped troubled companies restructure, and the employees of those companies often figured out why Sam was there. So, his clients' employees either had a healthy fear of him, or showered effusive kindness and information on him. They did *not* fire monster shots across the bow on day one right in the middle of the lunchroom. Sam immediately crowned Charlie the crazy uncle of the company.

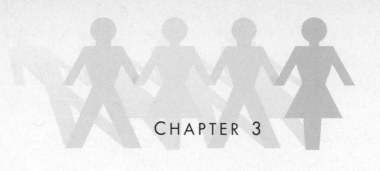

CHAPTER 3

NEIL DOWN

Sam's next stop was the Accounting Department. After interviewing the president of an organization, he always moved on to the financials. Neil, the CFO, greeted him with a suspect grin and they began chatting.

Neil had been CFO for nine years, and he looked the worse for wear. Probably in his late 40s, he was a heavy-set man who was a little shorter than average. He was prone to wear dress shirts that were too tight and ties that shined a little too much. He had thinning hair and an unkempt mustache. To Sam, it looked like Neil needed to wash his face once or twice with a soapy rag.

Some information was going to be difficult to cull or compile, and Neil made sure Sam knew that. Neil provided an initial pile of reporting, and Sam returned to his office to study it. Dick was right—the job costing models *did* look good. So why was the company bleeding? Sam went looking for Neil and found him standing in a hallway formed by rows of accounting cubicles on both sides.

"Neil, I've been reviewing your job cost modeling. When was the last time these were updated?"

"Sam, you can see the date. It's at the bottom of each report."

"So these are three years old. They're not current. Are you guys able to update them?"

"Are you *telling* me to update them?" Neil shot back.

"Neil, these won't prove to be of much use if they're inaccurate. I think that..."

"I don't have the time or resources to update this many models," Neil interjected. "Besides, not much has changed."

"Actually, margins have dipped quite a bit over the past..."

"Look, Sam, I need to get back to my office. We can discuss this more later," Neil said, before turning to walk away.

Strikeout. That didn't go well!

Neil got about 10 feet closer to his office before running into his controller, Josie. They had a brief conversation before Neil grew frustrated with her. As Josie was in mid-sentence, Neil swung his body 180 degrees, his more than ample frame sloshing to and fro, and began walking away. "Neil. Neil?" Josie said, but it was no use. He stormed back to his glass-walled office and slammed the door. It rebounded back open, and Josie knocked and followed him inside.

Sam watched the proceedings through the glass and tried to make out what was being said. Only the yelling was discernable. Josie was holding a report of some sort, and looked to be trying to explain herself. Neil was doing a lot of gesticulating and screaming. He grabbed the report out of Josie's hand, ripped it in half several times, and threw it back at her. The remnants started to separate above her head, and fell around her like oversized confetti.

She must have said something in response, because he then picked up his office phone and launched it across the room at her. She turned her body to avoid the projectile, causing it to crash to the floor a few feet behind her. "*Get outta here, you idiot!*" he yelled as he pointed at the door.

Josie exited Neil's office and stood outside his door for a second, looking more than a bit shocked. Her face turned beet red as she fought back the tears. She glanced to her left and to her right, catching the squinty, worried eyes of several accounting employees. Sam wanted to say something to her, but what might that be? He approached and talked with her for a few minutes before returning to his assigned office space to continue studying the information he had.

In the sparsely populated lunchroom, Sam saw Charlie across the way, and Charlie laser-locked eyes with him. Oh brother, here we go again.

"Hey Sam! Turkey tetrazzini today. Living high on the hog."

"Hi Charlie. Listen, I really need to work on some things for a bit. So..."

"Well, you can work on 'em and eat with me. Have a seat!" Sam really had no choice.

"How are things going in Accounting so far?" Charlie asked.

"I'm not sure. I just saw the weirdest thing."

"You talkin' about Neil?" Charlie asked.

"Yeah. How'd you know?"

"You know how it is at a company like this. Reputations get earned, gossip travels fast. What happened?"

"I was standing in Accounting, talking with Neil about his job costing models, and he cut me off mid-sentence. Said he had no time to talk. Then he just walked away. On his way back to his office, his controller, Josie, must've had some questions, because she stopped him. She's been here at Vunorri about three months. She was talking with Neil out in the cubicles, right among the staff accountants. She must've said something that offended him, because he got angry with her before turning around and walking away. He entered his office and slammed the door shut."

"What happened then?" asked Charlie.

"She followed him inside, and he threw a ripped up report at her. Then he chucked his office phone at her. Luckily, he missed. Is this normal behavior here?"

"She was brave to follow him in there," Charlie said. "Did you figure out what happened?"

"I talked to her afterward. She was crying. When he walked away, she thought it was just a misunderstanding. She was embarrassed that others had witnessed that. So she went in to try to explain herself, but it just infuriated him. He was very upset, obviously. She told me she thinks her job might be in jeopardy."

"Worried about her job and her boss nearly physically assaulted her," Charlie said. "Good reasons to be crying. Poor girl."

"Her job's not in jeopardy. Don't you think she's reaching there a bit?" Sam asked.

"No, I don't. Josie's young; she doesn't know any better. People get fired all the time for nothing. Neil's a seasoned veteran, and Josie's new to the company. Her boss just walked away in disgust, and threw stuff at her. She probably felt insignificant, disrespected, and terrified. Why take the time to make one of your employees feel that way? She's not sure of her standing at the company; she just started, and she's already getting office equipment thrown at her?"

Sam wanted to explain this away. "I'm sure Neil's just having…"

"Lest you think he's just having a bad day," Charlie interrupted, "this isn't the first time stuff like this has happened. He's always one step removed from insanity. He once yelled at an employee for an hour for investing two minutes of her afternoon to make a protein shake, claiming it was 'taking a second lunch.' He fired an employee for bringing him the wrong breakfast PowerBar. He storms out of meetings if he isn't getting his way. Managers aren't supposed to scream at people and storm out of meetings like some petulant child."

"But Charlie, why would Dick put up with such behavior?"

"Ask him yourself. Sam, Neil makes his employees *cry*. He's cruel. It's positively vile behavior. Working for him is a demoralizing slog. There's no joy in that department. Maybe he doesn't know any better, maybe he thinks he's getting results, I don't know. But here's the thing: he has a lot of institutional knowledge. He's been here so long and knows so much. As far as they're concerned, he's irreplaceable. As far as I'm concerned, that's simply not true."

"Why?" asked Sam.

"No one's irreplaceable. Now Sam, take note—that's *way* different than saying 'He'd be hard to replace,' or 'It would terribly inconvenient to spend the time to replace him.' Anything worth doing in life is going to be hard work. What's the tradeoff here? We get the use of his knowledge, but he throws phones and makes people cry? How is that OK?"

"I don't know," Sam said. "Neil's probably got a lot on his mind. Running a business is tough. You might not have much experience with this. I mean, it's just life at work. I'm sure it was nothing personal."

Charlie put his foot down. "It is *not* OK. You're sanctioning poor behavior by believing, 'It's not personal; it's just business.' This isn't *The Godfather*—Vunorri's a real-life business with real human beings working at it. Of course it's personal. It's always personal. These celebrated, archetype 'tough' bosses need to become a relic of the past. They're old and busted. Being kind and considerate to others is the new hotness."

"Pardon me for saying," Sam said, "but aren't you a little 'seasoned' to be saying 'new hotness'?"

Charlie smiled. "Grandkids. Listen, I want to see this kind of boss marginalized, gone from the landscape. We should stop justifying their behavior and glorifying their ill-gotten gains. No, you're not a tough boss. You're just an abusive jerk.

"And employees crying? There's nothing wrong with a good cry, depending on circumstances. But crying at work...Sam, those tears should speak to you. Bosses who make people cry are nothing but blunt instruments. When it comes to dealing with employees, we can do better. I learned a long time ago—if your job is making you cry yourself to sleep at night, get outta there! Find the escape hatch and jump in! Crying in bed? Bed is for sleeping, making love, and eating the occasional sandwich. We have George Costanza to thank for that."

"Charlie, you might be a few sandwiches short of a picnic, but you have an interesting take on the workplace."

Sam returned to his office and the piles of financial reports. He spent the afternoon pouring over what Neil had provided. Where were the inefficiencies that were resulting in these slipping margins? And why were the job costing models so old and so wrong? Worse, why wouldn't Neil want to help the cause? Finally, why wouldn't Dick demand better from him?

Sam needed more information if he was going to get to the bottom of it all. Right then, it occurred to him that Dick gave him no instructions on *whom* to contact in each department. If Neil wanted to barricade himself in his office, maybe Josie and her direct reports could help.

CHAPTER 4

WORK MADNESS

SAM'S BEST-LAID PLANS WERE A SWING AND A MISS.

He returned to the Accounting Department the next day and met with fierce resistance and pronounced grumpiness. Sam usually had the magic touch with people and interviews, but not so here. He chalked it up to the insanities of the previous day.

Nevertheless, he was frustrated, so he decided to switch gears and head out to the warehouse to introduce himself to Rod, the warehouse manager. Time to start scheduling warehouse interviews. He found Rod near the packing line.

"Rod, hey, I'm Sam. The consultant Dick brought in."

Rod was one of the few bright spots at Vunorri. He was a level-headed, talented fellow. He had attended college but never graduated. Instead, he came to Vunorri and worked his way up the ladder over 12 years. He had a way with people, which was incredibly difficult to pull off at Vunorri. He was definitely swimming upstream, but had never considered leaving, as he was a fiercely loyal employee. For him, the grass could have been greener on the other side, but he wanted to turn Vunorri's grass green.

"Hi, Sam. Nice to meet you," he said in a tremulous tone. "Listen, umm...I'll be with you in a few minutes. There's something I need to take care of first." Sam nodded in approval.

Out of the left corner of his eye, Sam saw Dick storm into the warehouse with a tornadic speed that screamed, *"I mean business!"* Then, sure enough, he began screaming.

"Rod! Get over here!" Dick shouted as he charged at Rod, arms flying in all directions in order to give his point more flourish. "What in God's green earth is going on in this warehouse? What is the matter with you people? You're gettin' soft out here! It's like you're asleep at the wheel! I am sick of all the packing errors. Sick of the mess out here. This truck hasn't been unloaded. These pallets haven't been put up in the racking. I've had enough! What are you gonna do about the errors?"

"Sir, we're double-checking most outgoing orders now to cut down on the..."

"Well, it had better work! Get things humming out here, real quick, or you're gonna be lookin' for a job! Got it? Shape it up, now!"

Dick then exited the warehouse as fast as he had entered, and Rod's employees began to act busy again, pretending they had not been listening. Rod ran his hand through his hair, looking deflated as he slowly walked back to where Sam was standing.

"What was that all about?" Sam asked.

"Shhhhh. Hey, come over here," Rod said as he led Sam over to a quieter spot near one of the outer walls.

"Don't worry," Rod said. "Dick wasn't really mad. We staged the whole thing."

"You did what now?" Sam said, quite puzzled.

"It wasn't real. We made the whole thing up."

"You mean that tirade was fake? Why?"

"We're not performing up to expectations out here. Errors are up. Slower throughput rates. People coming in late. I'm having a hard time hitting numbers. Dick knows they respect me, so if he lets me have it within earshot of them, they usually get the message and perk up."

"So it works?" Sam asked.

Rod hesitated a moment before answering. "It works *for us*," shrugging his shoulders as if resigned to his fate. "It's one of Dick's tactics, and it works for Dick. It is what it is."

Sam looked around the warehouse and saw employees with a bit more pep in their step.

"You OK, Rod? You look a little shaken."

"Yeah, I'm OK."

"I mean, the whole thing was fake, so..."

"It still isn't easy," Rod admitted.

Rod didn't seem to be in top form, so Sam wanted to get out of his hair for the day. "Tell you what. I wanna get some stuff on the schedule with you and your people. I can come back later."

It was as if Charlie worked two jobs—mailroom worker and lunchroom philosopher. There he was again.

"Sam, you look troubled," Charlie said. "And hungry."

"It's been an interesting day so far. My friends in Accounting weren't too friendly this morning."

"What do you need their help for?" Charlie asked.

"Well, if you must know, I'm conducting a complete financial study of the organization, and to do so, I need all of the pertinent information. Accounting is the only place to get the info. I probably shouldn't be telling you any of this, but Neil's not being very forthcoming, and his people are walking on eggshells."

"Maybe it's you," Charlie surmised.

"What do you mean?" Sam asked. "I think it's just because of what happened yesterday."

"Are you sure?" Charlie asked. "Think about it. You've been hired to 'shake things up' and get this place profitable again. What do you think your presence means to these people?"

"Well...I guess they could consider me a threat. For instance, I could recommend layoffs. I might recommend specific layoffs."

"Sooooooo, why didn't they help you this morning?" Charlie asked.

Charlie's pushy inquiries tweaked Sam. "That's a great question! They should want me to like them so I don't recommend laying them off. They should want me to determine they're not unnecessary. Maybe they should *care* about the company."

"Sam, many of these people do care. Some of them want to do great work. And almost all of them *need* this job. In case you were unaware, losing one's job can prove devastating. People here don't feel like they have any mobility. I mean, what job are they gonna go get? We're one of two manufacturers in town. The economy is a mess. All of this depresses them even more. That's a downward spiral you don't wanna get caught up in. It's not a healthy way for these people to live. So they're just really nervous to have someone like you around.

"Plus," Charlie continued, "I don't think the Great Recession ever ended. Downward pressure on earnings and increased competition are stressing the heck out of people like Dick. America has 8%

unemployment, and Europe would kill for that number. Meanwhile, civility is on a *rapid* decline. We can't seem to find a way to get along, Sam—not at work, in politics, religion, even at home."

"Get along?" Sam asked. "At work? You'd be surprised how little that matters. You think about a lot of weird stuff."

"You never think about such things? You don't watch the news and see 1% vs. 99%? This sort of thing doesn't trouble you? Doesn't make you think?"

"Sure, I watch the news," Sam said. "Why should I care? I fail to see what class warfare has to do with Vunorri."

"Well, I suppose you noticed...the world has never been more divided, except maybe during World War II. We're a bunch of *"me me me"* individuals running around only caring about ourselves. And if we do team up, it's to fend off or defeat opposing groups, or—and think about this—it's because working at a company *forces us* into a collective. Employer vs. employee is like a veritable cage match right now. How is that good for the health of the workplace?"

"You know, Charlie? You're a lotta fun to have lunch with."

"Hey, I didn't promise smiles. Just some company and maybe a little wisdom you need to hear."

"Well, why don't the people here at Vunorri get along?" Sam asked in a skeptical tone.

"So many reasons. But here's the quickest explanation: too much has happened to forget. People here have been mistreating each other, doing both the little things that annoy and the big things that cause major riffs, for a long time. This place needs a lot more nice."

"So what can be done about it?" Sam asked.

"Someone needs to make the first move here," Charlie said. "Someone has to say sorry *first*, so to speak."

"Say sorry?" Sam asked.

"We need to stop fighting with each other over the personal, intrinsic differences *that will always be present!* Our employees need to walk in each other's shoes and accept their differences in wealth, race, talent, ambition, and cultural beliefs."

"Good luck with *that*," Sam quipped.

"...and it all starts with Dick," Charlie said. "Crazy companies are usually crazy because of leadership. They set the tone."

"What's crazy about this place?" Sam asked. "Vunorri's just struggling through market forces, maybe top-heavy on employees. What's so crazy?"

Charlie leaned forward with a wise grin and said, "How long ya got?"

"Try me."

Charlie rubbed his hands together, as if preparing to lay it down.

"Well, let's start with what you witnessed today."

"What are you talking about?" Sam asked.

"In the warehouse."

Sam stared at Charlie, trying to figure out if they were talking about the same thing.

"You know," Charlie said. "Dick and Rod's little Shakespeare play?"

"How do you know about that?"

"Bad news travels fast. You saw it, right?"

"I saw the whole thing," Sam said. "And I have to say, it was some kind of a genius idea."

"Genius?" Charlie responded. "You *like* this? Let me tell you something—there was a better way. The purposeful addition of stress to a work environment is completely avoidable. Unacceptable."

"Hey, did it work?"

"Who cares?" Charlie said. "Was there a better way to achieve the same result without yelling? Of course there was. You might think you saw results after the screaming ended, but do you know what you missed? You missed how those employees felt afterward. How much stress they had running through their veins. How they feared for their jobs. How they took that stress home. How their families were subjected to that stress. So unnecessary. Why use fear and intimidation? Why do you have to scare us? This isn't a haunted house."

"You didn't answer me. Did it work?"

"You're asking the wrong question," Charlie said. "I could go out and rob 10 rich people at gunpoint, and I will have met with a very handsome financial return. 'Did it work?' In fact, the ROI of robbing people would seemingly be infinity, since I put nothing into the project. Well, maybe some sweat equity and the cost of the gun."

"You're saying the end doesn't justify the means," Sam said.

"Why not just speak to the employees? Why not tell them what you want, and by when you want it? Give them clear expectations."

"Look Charlie, sometimes work isn't a lovey-dovey cakewalk of smiles and happiness. I don't know how you like to motivate people, but doves and olive branches don't always do the trick. Dick and Rod needed to get the attention of the warehouse workers. If a shot across the bow means Rod's employees got the message, then it worked."

"It's a shame you think that way," Charlie said. "These are *people* we're dealing with here. Why do we treat our loved ones with kid gloves, and then come to work and treat people like property—like inanimate objects, replaceable parts? Those warehouse people had a terrible morning today, and it didn't have to be so. Their attentiveness was dearly bought."

Sam considered Charlie's position. He wondered if Charlie had ever been in charge of anything, because it didn't seem like he knew what it took to run a business.

"You got anything else?" Sam asked.

Charlie had something for him that had nothing to do with nefarious management tactics. "Dick had a mini-meltdown recently that was actually genuine. His top lieutenants were coming in 5, 10, 30 minutes late. Sometimes they'd stay three hours late, but Dick didn't care. Things felt loosey goosey to him, so during their weekly management meeting, he sternly laid down some new rules. Start time at Vunorri was 8:00 a.m. sharp. Be on time!

"Dick tends to repeat himself when he's trying to drive home a point, which can be kind of funny. He kept saying, 'I am sick and tired of people floating in and out of this place. If I'm going to run a successful company, we have to have rules! Eight o'clock is go time.' So according to Dick, no more getting here at 8:05."

This made sense to Sam. Show up on time. If that's what Dick wants, do it.

"The next day—the very next day!—when did Dick arrive at work? He rolled in at 9:45. He didn't have an appointment out of the office. Didn't call in to let anyone know where he was. Just showed up almost two hours late. His managers looked at each other like 'why?' Same old Dick."

"Charlie, maybe he was working from home, or maybe he really was at an offsite meeting. You never know. Company leaders are busy."

"Sam, don't ask your employees to do anything that you wouldn't do yourself. Dick set a *terrible* example by showing up late one day after his little tirade. How do you think that made everyone feel? I won't make you answer, but I can tell you for a fact—not good. Same old Vunorri."

Sam believed in Dick and go-getters like him—the entrepreneurs of the world, the risk-takers, the producers, and the moneymakers. He again concluded that Charlie was grasping at little straws.

Charlie was unfazed. "Well let's see, which story will win the day for me? There's the customer service manager yelling at a customer while pretending to be the owner of Vunorri. He got a slap on the wrist for that. There's the HR director dressing down a fellow manager in a company-wide meeting for having mispronounced the name of a competitor. There's Dick making the receptionist drive him to the mall to buy underwear."

Sam looked at Charlie quizzically and did that special trick where you raise one eyebrow.

"I'm serious!" Charlie said. "Dick needed underwear, but he had recently undergone a medical procedure. Doctor's orders, he wasn't supposed to drive. So he made the receptionist drive him to the mall. Two hours to buy underwear! Someone had to come up and cover the phones."

"These stories seem like minor annoyances, Charlie. I don't see what they have to do with the numbers."

"If I can make an observation...it seems you're a bit too obsessed with numbers and winning to care about people," Charlie said.

"Again, why should I care?"

"Really?"

"Really," Sam confirmed. "It's just a job. They care about their pay, their job title, and taking vacations. They care about themselves. They don't care about me, and they don't care about little aggravations at work."

Charlie got serious again. "You're very much missing my point. If you, Sam, are somehow able to keep the president of the company from stealing employees away to go buy some new tighty whiteys, yeah, maybe you aren't gonna be the hero who saves Vunorri. I get that. But all of this stupid stuff adds up over time. People don't realize that. Negativity collects like plaque on teeth. You can't look in the mirror in the morning and see plaque forming. All of a sudden, it's just there, and the dental hygienist is cranking on your teeth with that awful tool. Like I told you the other day, enough has happened here over time that the snowball rolling down the hill is huge!"

Charlie looked at Sam as if to say, "You're not quite grasping this, are you?" Sam shot him a look back that said, "You're not quite carrying your argument."

Every workplace in the world had these problems, but many of those companies were excelling financially. Why couldn't Charlie accept that? Charlie then proffered an idea that Sam didn't reject out of hand.

"Sam, the worst part of it is that we have some good people. Rod's a good manager—not many other good managers, but hey, at least we have one! And yeah, we have some knucklehead employees, but we have some *great* people, too. Frankly, I don't know why they're still here.

"They get *no* support. No 'Open Door policy' here at Vunorri. It's 'Closed Door!' Managers do *not* want you to come and see them. Their M.O. is 'Don't bring me any surprises.' Our employees are out on the front lines. They're the ones most able to diagnose problems and suggest improvements. On the other hand, our managers have the college educations and fancy job titles, so they must know more than us about solving business issues, right? But, instead of getting their hands dirty, they sequester themselves up in The Tower and run this place into the ground. What a horrible way to construct a business."

"The Tower?" Sam asked.

"Yup. That's the fourth floor. All of the top managers, including Dick, spend most of their time up there. Even your friend Neil has a second office in The Tower. He splits time between his two offices, depending on his mood. A few years ago, someone started calling it 'The Tower' and the name stuck. Gives it a perfect air of exclusivity, if you ask me."

Sam returned to his office, leaned back in his chair and stared out the window. Accounting was practically stonewalling him. If there was a financial needle in a haystack here at Vunorri, he was going to need to find it. And during most consulting engagements, it usually wasn't *that* hard to find.

So why had he just wasted two hours having lunch with Charlie the populist? Story after story about downtrodden workers and evil management...and Charlie almost seemed to enjoy the fight. How could a lazy, unskilled workforce like Vunorri's ever help these managers turn the company around? Charlie and his friends from the left side of the political fence were so concerned about what goes on in "The Tower," but were they even trying to do their jobs well? The so-called "crazy" stories Charlie shared were not atypical—all businesses have this stuff. It doesn't matter how wacky a workplace is, Sam thought. What matters are margins and profits.

Sam wrote in his notebook:

> *"Charlie might be a good mail jockey who can spin a story, but he most certainly doesn't know what it takes to run a business."*

CHAPTER 5

SHARED RESPONSIBILITY

"*BLAAAAAARGHH*, THAT'S AWFUL!"

With Charlie nowhere in sight, Sam took a seat in the lunchroom alone for a quick bite to eat. He wanted a little Friday peace and quiet after an eventful first week. Across the way, a few workers—either factory or warehouse—were already well into their lunches. All of a sudden, one of them stood up and violently spit out the food he had in his mouth.

"Dude, what's wrong?" asked one of his lunch mates. "Are you choking?"

"*No!* I just bit into something gross. What *was* that???" He proceeded to run straight to the bathroom. The commotion must have been Charlie's bat signal. There were doings-a-transpirin'!

"What was that all about?" Charlie asked as he entered the lunchroom. Sam was in no mood to hang out with Charlie, but circumstances dictated otherwise.

"The guy ate some dessert that didn't agree with him," Sam said.

"It wasn't by chance a Little Debbie Oatmeal Crème Pie, was it?"

"Come to think of it," Sam said, "that's what it looked like. How did you know that?" Charlie did have a way of baiting a hook.

"Well, we've been having some theft problems here in the lunchroom fridge. People's lunches keep disappearing. We've kinda suspected it might be those guys, but no one's ever caught 'em in the act. A little birdie told me that some employees decided to take matters into their own hands. They threw some brown bag lunches in there with a few surprises."

"Charrrrrrlie?"

"Sam, it wasn't me. This is just what I heard. One of the surprises might've been a Little Debbie Oatmeal Crème Pie with an industrial alteration—the crème in the middle was replaced with white caulk." For a brief moment, Sam didn't know what to think. But he had been a prankster as a kid, so it brought back some good memories.

"I have to admit," Sam said. "That's kinda funny!"

"It's hard not to laugh, right?" Charlie said. "The guy got his comeuppance. The only problem is that hungry employees are having their lunches stolen. Management has done just about everything they can, short of removing the fridge, but the thefts continue." Sam wasn't sure he heard Charlie correctly.

"Charlie, for a moment there, you sounded like a downright reasonable man. You mean management *isn't* to blame for this?" Sam asked rather sarcastically.

"Sam, during our lunches over the past week, I don't remember ever taking a pro-vigilante poisoning position! While we're having a little laugh at those knuckleheads' expense, I'd rather Vunorri employees stop stealing from each other, and it would probably be best if employees weren't trying to poison each other. I know I'm staking out brave territory here. But shenanigans like this just make management's job harder."

"Are you sure you're not Charlie's smarter twin?"

Sam's view of the workplace was from the top down—management struggling to control the workforce and extracting from them what they need. He assumed that Charlie's view was from the bottom up. That's all he had heard to date—management oppressing its workers. Sam should not have assumed anything.

"Sam, let me ask you a question. You believe in management and their goals and good intentions, correct?" Sam nodded. "And you believe, to some degree, that employees are worthy of nothing less than rigid control, as they're prone to be lazy, make mistakes...basically they're out to squeeze as much blood from the turnip as possible, right?" Sam agreed.

"OK, let me ask you this. When a company is struggling financially...when people aren't getting along...when no one wants to come to work...don't you think that both sides are to blame? Shouldn't both management and workers share the responsibility?"

Charlie was headed in a direction that Sam instinctually didn't want to go—complexity. Sam understood black and white, but Charlie was swimming in the deep end of the grays.

"Sam, I'll *prove* to you I'm not bent or biased. Our management team has its obvious shortcomings, but how much harder do they have to work because of some of the goofballs they have to manage? So, go do some interviews and find out more about these people I'm about to tell you about, OK?"

Sam wasn't sure he should be spending this much time at this juncture listening to the old man spin the yarn, but he was trapped. Charlie began his dissertation.

"We had an employee out in the warehouse that our manager Rod could often not locate. Eventually the guy would turn up and claim he had been in the bathroom. Turns out he had been in there all right—he'd lock the door and smoke dope for 30 minutes before heading back to his post. So Rod fired him.

"Then the guy filed for unemployment, and Rod fought it—he didn't want Vunorri to be on the hook for the guy's unemployment benefits, as we fired him for cause. The Department of Labor awarded this pothead unemployment. How much harder do we all have to work so this dude can get high on the job? The guy was a clown and should've been fired long ago."

"Well, I'm glad there are people like Rod here," Sam said. "People who care about their duty."

Charlie continued. "Then there's the curious case of one of our factory workers, Dale, who is easily the most error-prone employee we have. Nice guy, but he constantly makes mistakes; he can't help himself. He insists that he checks his work—"double-checked and triple-checked"—that's what he always says. But the errors continue. Others have to redo his work and cover for him all the time. Managers and fellow employees have tried to help this guy out, but it's no use. Why is he still here?

"How about our receptionist? She must live some sort of hard life, because she often falls asleep at the front desk. So people—well, *some* people—are busting their butts here, and she's at the front desk sawing logs. What a great impression she's making on visitors, too! And again, managers have told her to remain awake, as if that's something they should have to tell her.

"And just about every employee with Internet access abuses the privilege. Social media use on the job is rampant. Our IT department should lock it down, or managers should make sure their people are delivering results. But no, the abuse continues. Some people here are so lazy. You know, there's a guy somewhere deep in a mine, digging coal out of the ground so that our employees can play Farmville and Candy Crush Saga at work." Sam couldn't help but let a laugh escape.

"And, Sam, I saved this one for last, just for you. One of our customer service reps, Tina, loves to chit-chat with the customers she has on the phone. Normally that would be a value-add, but in her case, it can be a hot mess. She's lewd and loud—too loud, so people around her can really hear her conversations. Like the time she was talking on the phone to a customer about her period." Sam almost blew Dr. Pepper out of his nose.

"*What*?" he exclaimed.

"Everyone heard it," Charlie said. "That's pretty unprofessional, right? You can't say stuff like that to a customer! She actually got reprimanded that time. It didn't seem to help. She's still demonstrating poor judgment, both with her fellow employees and customers on the phone.

"Everyone has to work harder to cover for these people and for the managers who won't replace them. And pardon these good employees for not wanting to work harder, but for them, it's an issue of fairness. Their nonperforming coworkers are dead weight. Some of them have no desire to improve. And management sometimes tries to help, but rarely pulls the trigger on termination. We only lose people during layoffs, or when a manager is in a bad mood. See how complicated the solution *really* is? We can't affect positive change unless *everyone* steps up."

"I do find it interesting," Sam said, "that you failed to mention these pro-owner feelings earlier."

"Well," Charlie said, "You didn't ask. Besides, they're not pro-owner. That's the key to the whole thing, Sam! There are situations *every single day* where management and workers need to cooperate.

Yet, as far as I can tell, anything goes here at Vunorri. Management could maybe do more to improve things, but employees need not run wild just because they *can*. Management as 'zookeeper' isn't a sustainable work model.

"Responsibility runs both ways, Sam. Neither side wants to hear that, but it just does. It rarely makes sense to take one side and push that side's agenda to the bitter end. How can we take the side of workers and not keep in mind the needs of ownership and management? How can we give management all of the bullets and forget the needs of the entry-level worker?

"So you see, if we're losing the battle, it's because we're not cooperating. Our failure here at Vunorri is one that management and rank and file can celebrate together. We share in it equally. It's frustrating to me that people here aren't more self-motivated. An employee has no one but themselves to blame for not trying harder."

Sam arrived at home and went straight to his office to sort through the day. He hadn't unearthed any financial smoking guns that would satisfy the bank, but he had much to think about. He paged through his notes and zeroed in on one little phrase:

"Maybe not entirely crazy"

Charlie, the self-appointed wise old sage of Vunorri...Sam still considered him to be cuckoo and a little "left field," as Charlie seemed to focus 100% of his work philosophy on human beings, with little regard to the lifeblood of business: profits. He still wasn't entirely sure what to make of Mr. Mailroom, but upon further review he realized he might have been interacting with his intellectual equal. That alone piqued his interest. He was drawn to the man. Further complicating matters, Charlie had revealed a reasonable, nuanced side of himself. Responsibility runs both ways? Sam was not going to be able to make this the cornerstone of any presentation to Dick or the bank. However, he wasn't sure he should continue to completely dismiss the old man. After all, he *was* learning quite a bit about the company, and that's why he chatted up employees in the first place. Through the muck, Charlie was good intel.

Sam finished jotting down and organizing his notes from the week. It had been a rougher ride than he had anticipated, and he hadn't even met the Antichrist of Human Resources yet.

CHAPTER 6

WORK AS A CORTISOL TRAGEDY

WEEK TWO STARTED WITH A SUNNY MONDAY MORNING AND a packed agenda. Upon arriving at Vunorri, Sam plopped his belongings in his assigned office and walked to the lunchroom for coffee. Crap—no one had made coffee yet. He knew he should have stopped on the way to work. As if Charlie felt a disturbance in The Force, he magically materialized before Sam's eyes in the lunchroom doorway.

"Good morning Sam! What's your plan for this week?"

"I'm with Human Resources first. I'm still not sure about later this week."

"Ha! You're going to meet our HR Director, Melinda! Have you met her yet?"

"No," Sam responded.

"Hold on to your seat, my friend. Strap yourself in and feel the burn! *Nothing* can prepare you for her."

"Oh come on. How bad could she be?" Sam asked. "This isn't gonna be like Hell Week with the Navy Seals. Relax."

"OK, you're the boss," Charlie responded. "Good luck. And in the coming days, I imagine we'll have something to talk about over lunch."

Sam began interviewing Human Resources personnel, and would meet with the supposedly infamous Melinda tomorrow. During this day's interviews, he heard some surprisingly frank HR employees brazenly revealing many dangerous practices utilized in the organization. He wondered why they were being so candid.

"Sam, won't you join me?" Charlie asked.

"Lunch just wouldn't be the same," Sam deadpanned.

In a mini plot twist, Sam actually wanted to confide in Charlie, or at least ask his opinion about one particular quirk the HR interviews had revealed. But, he didn't even want to admit to himself that he wanted to talk to Charlie. In Sam's eyes, Charlie was just too batty. And he had never before had this many conversations with one employee. Still, the alternative was to go talk to...whom?

"Charlie, can I run something by you?"

"Shoot!"

"Today I was interviewing some of Melinda's people. What is The Notebook?"

"Isn't that a movie that women like?" Charlie joked. "Ryan Gosling—what a hunk."

"Funny. Seriously, what's this notebook all about?"

"They told you about The Notebook, huh?" Charlie looked surprised. Everyone knew about The Notebook, but it remained one of those office oddities, unspoken of by most. Unless you were in it—and then you just worried about it.

"In a typical organization," Charlie continued, "Human Resources maintains personnel files. Performance reviews are sometimes kept in those files; some organizations purposely keep such things out of personnel files. Here? Melinda keeps a notebook. Well, not on everyone. On the troublesome employees. Or the ones she thinks are trouble."

"What's in this notebook?" Sam asked.

"Didn't her people tell you?"

"No. They said to ask her tomorrow."

"Well," Charlie explained, "The Notebook contains a list of the things she thinks you're doing wrong. Then, if she desires, you have to meet with her on a weekly basis to discuss The Notebook."

"Huh?" Sam said.

Charlie explained that Dick most likely knew nothing about The Notebook. That's how far out of touch he was. Melinda was a stern taskmaster. She had Dick's ear, because she exuded power and made Dick's life easier. She dealt with it all, so he didn't have to.

"The other thing, Sam, is that I don't think our HR department fears anyone. They don't fear you. They don't fear Dick. They are strong, and everyone else is weak. It's just another part of the rich tapestry that makes up Vunorri."

Sam was having trouble computing what he was hearing. "I can understand conducting performance reviews," he said. "Probationary action plans, performance improvement plans, progressively punitive discipline...I've seen all that before. But a notebook? Weekly discussions about what you're doing wrong?"

"I told you she was nuts," Charlie said. "Certifiable. I didn't oversell her, did I? And you haven't even met her yet! Have you found out about *how* we lay people off? If not, ask her."

"I've seen a lot in my time," Sam said, "but this is a first."

"Sam, have you ever stopped to consider the lunacy of the workplace?"

"OK," Sam responded, "this is where I'm supposed to say 'What do you mean?' So..."

"The whole thing's just...well, *tragic*. Robert Frost once wrote, 'The brain is a wonderful organ; it starts working the moment you get up in the morning and does not stop until you get into the office.' Unfortunately, all too often true. Vunorri presents its employees with a progression of little bad things that happen, often with big, hairy problems mixed in.

"Think about it. We go to work because we need to support ourselves and our families. We have caviar dreams about making tons of money—we want to make lots of money! That's what we think we *need*. So we get a job, and we're happy at first. We have hope. We're happy on the first day, during the first week—the honeymoon period.

"Then the politics, the backbiting, the cliques, the strife, the piles of work, the buck-passing, the people different than us. You start to get to know the players. If you actually wanted to excel, to learn more about your craft, forget it. You're too busy bickering about the dumbest things. We treat each other poorly, as means to an end or as expendable tools, rather than human beings.

"All of this is stressful. Stress releases cortisol into the brain. Cortisol is a stress hormone, as you might've guessed. Sometimes we begin experiencing chronic stress and significant physiological changes. Whoa, that's kind of scary, isn't it? At this point, most of our human needs are going unmet. This causes more cortisol to be released.

"It's at this genius moment when our superiors normally pull a stressed person aside and ask them to shape up, or 'Just relax.' Telling an upset person to relax is utterly pointless! My wife taught me that years ago," Charlie said with a wink.

"Often, we begin protecting ourselves—our position at the job—by lashing out, not getting along with others, building up our walls and defenses. We're a thousand defense mechanisms and no empathy. We do stuff to people at work that we'd never consider doing to a friend or loved one. Remember, this builds upon itself like plaque on teeth, like a snowball rolling down a hill.

"So, Sam, let me ask you. What do you think this does to our work teams?"

Sam knew where Charlie was going, but hated letting him score points. Nevertheless, he played along. "It inhibits their success?"

"Exactly! If you can't work well with others, it's very difficult to excel. And if you don't have teams of people excelling at their jobs, Vunorri Inc. isn't operating at peak efficiency. Not even close! Things aren't getting done, or improved. No productivity, no raises, no kindness, no fulfillment, no happiness. Terrible! No wonder the bank has a noose around our neck."

Sam uncomfortably sat still, silently breathing through his nose. How did Charlie know about the bank?

"Sam, do you understand what I'm meaning to say?" Charlie asked. "Vunorri Inc. takes perfectly good employees and reduces them to rubble."

"Oh nonsense. They're just hiring the wrong people."

"Maybe a few, but we're hiring lots of good people, too, and this place crushes them. Be careful, Sam. Stay here long enough and it could happen to you."

Sam let out a sarcastic laugh. "Sorry Charlie, not gonna happen. This isn't my first rodeo. I've been doing turnarounds for years, been in a lot of toxic environments. I've walked into some dreadful situations. A month here isn't gonna take me off my game."

"I'm glad you believe in yourself," Charlie said. "Glad you're happy in your line of work, too."

"Strong people can work their way through anything," Sam said. "Maybe Vunorri needs more people cut from that cloth."

"Sam, I don't want you to get the wrong idea. Vunorri isn't always doom and gloom. Sometimes circumstances present themselves, or rather, they thrust themselves upon us, and you really get to see the promise some of our people have.

"A few years ago, we had our main server crash. It was an old unit, and the hard drive locked up. So we hustled in a replacement machine and went to our nightly backup tape. It was blank. Blank! The backups had not been running. So we took the hard drive to a local lab; nothing on it was recoverable. They had to send it to a clean room in California.

"This put us in an incredible bind. The server controlled everything except the phones. It had all of our receivables, payables, and inventory. It spit out pick tickets for the warehouse, cut sheets for raw materials processing—it did everything. We were basically shut down, about to lose tens of thousands of dollars.

"So Rod and a few of the guys got together and came up with an ingenious temporary fix. They created a rudimentary facsimile of our system using Microsoft Excel. Order entry punched in the details of incoming orders, and this automatically created documents for manufacturing, the warehouse, invoicing and accounting. We were back up and running by the next day. Their determination saved us."

"Wow," Sam said. He genuinely found that interesting.

"They stayed here till the wee hours of the morning working on it. I think they even had a few beers while toiling away. It was fun for them—one of those rays of sunshine at a place that's normally very cloudy. Do you understand what happened? They put aside their petty politics, disagreements, and grievances and worked together *with purpose.* They were unstoppable, and quite happy to have contributed to the cause. Happy during a crisis! This kind of happiness is rare here, but I believe we could duplicate it.

"Sam, if you want Vunorri's employees to excel, so they're operating on all cylinders and making Dick money, you need to embrace an unconventional view of productivity and profit. The real change you need to demand is the creation of a happy place to work. And that doesn't start with money, or power, or manufacturing tactics. It's about humans working in harmony, with purpose."

"You are a *fascinating* man, Charlie."

"Sam, can I give you a piece of advice?"

Sam looked at Charlie curiously. "Well so far I haven't been able to stop you, right?"

"You wanna see how some of this works?" Charlie asked. "Do you want to understand my point about teamwork, profit, and happiness? Tomorrow, get here early and brew the coffee."

"*That's* your advice?" Sam asked incredulously.

"Yes. Tomorrow, make the coffee. Hold open a few doors for people. Smile at someone. See what happens."

Sam still didn't believe any of this hocus-pocus happiness stuff moved the bottom line even a twitch, and he'd probably just wait until someone else made the coffee.

PART TWO

RESPECT FOR EACH OTHER: HUMAN SOLIDARITY

"Human solidarity demands that we look upon each other as brothers and sisters."
—CHRISTOPHER HITCHENS

"Kindness in words creates confidence. Kindness in thinking creates profoundness. Kindness in giving creates love."
—LAO TZU

"What was once impossible now summons us to dismantle the walls between ourselves and our sisters and brothers, to dissolve the distinctions between flesh and spirit, to transcend the present limits of time and matter, to find, at last, not wealth or power but the ecstasy *(so long forgotten)* of commonplace, unconditional being."
—GEORGE B. LEONARD

CHAPTER 7

THE ANTICHRIST OF HR

"Hello, Sam. Have a seat."

Today was Melinda day. In the entirety of Sam's career, never had a single meeting been accompanied by such a suspenseful buildup. Charlie depicted Melinda as the devil incarnate, and the previous day's interviews with her employees provided hints of trouble. Sam had hundreds of similar interviews under his belt, but he was nonetheless nervous. Not peeing-in-your-pants nervous, but definitely apprehensive.

Melinda looked to be in her mid-40s. She was rather tall and razor thin. Bony, but wiry and a little muscular at the same time—she took care of herself.

Sam thought about strategy for the meeting and decided he was going to have to go in heavy, weapons hot, to get the information he wanted. If Melinda wanted a fight, she'd get one. This is how you deal with such people.

"I hope you're well prepared," Melinda said. "I don't have all day."

For the next three hours, Sam peppered Melinda with questions about layoffs, performance evaluations, onboarding, training, and more. Sam's questions were met with sneers, derision, and bickering.

Melinda was testy, but in control. And she was agitating Sam, which might have been her plan.

While figuratively pulling these teeth, Sam learned about and took notes on the following:

- Due to lackluster financial results, Vunorri had executed three rounds of layoffs over the past five years. The first round included gathering the people being laid off in a conference room, luring them there under the auspices of a meeting invite. They were made to wait for about 45 minutes or so, until Melinda arrived to lower the boom—they were all being terminated, effective immediately. While they were sequestered, HR personnel were stripping down their cubes, emptying their lockers, and boxing up their stuff. The affected workers were told they would not be allowed to go back to their desks (or the warehouse or factory). They were handed their box of belongings and escorted to the parking lot under the watchful supervision of some rather muscular guys.

- About a year later, as the financial picture continued to darken, there was a second round of layoffs. The first round had caused some hurt feelings and poor morale. Apparently, the dismissals were too sudden, affected workers were not given a proper chance to say goodbye to anyone, and people did not appreciate having all of their personal belongings touched and handled by others. So Melinda and her team devised a new strategy. Thirty people were called into a meeting and told that, in one week's time, exactly half of them would be getting laid off. They were not told which 15 would be staying and which 15 would be going. This resulted in all 30 people spending a week on pins and needles, wondering whether they'd have jobs or not. After a week, HR kept its promise and informed 15 of them that the party was over. The 15 workers not losing their jobs watched as the displaced 15, their friends and work comrades, packed up and walked out, sullen and humiliated.

- Two years later, more layoffs were necessary, so a third round of cuts was planned. Human Resources considered how to handle it this time, as the second round of layoffs had provided some additional teaching moments. They learned that people didn't enjoy being laid off in the presence of coworkers, as it was humiliating (a lesson apparently not learned during round one). Also, the week of suspense and waiting was overly stressful and depressed the productivity of the 30 people *and* the people who worked with them. Finally, the 15 who did not lose their jobs were appropriately traumatized by the experience, and either regressed in their performance or quit. The strategy for this third round was therefore altered to rip the Band-Aid off as quickly as possible. Human Resources e-mailed a group of 30 people on a Sunday morning and informed them they had been laid off, effective immediately, and to not come to work the next day. They were promised a home delivery of their personal belongings. Unfortunately, not everyone checked their e-mail on Sunday, and some of the affected workers showed up on Monday and started working. Melinda quickly caught word of this and had them escorted from the building.

- Sam had heard of several instances where sick employees were forced to return to work, and Melinda confirmed this. "We didn't have time for a few employees to get the sniffles." Employees were also prohibited from leaving to attend to their sick kids, for ostensibly similar reasons.

- Sam learned that some factory workers routinely exceeded 40 hours worked in a week but had not been paid overtime. Melinda countered that overtime was not deserved as the employees had been converted to salaried workers. Sam knew well that this was likely a violation of labor law.

- Melinda and her team rarely consulted HR attorneys for assistance on challenging employment matters. Even though there was not a legal expert among them, Vunorri's HR department unilaterally made the decisions they thought best for the company.

- Sam found performance write-ups—first and second warnings for all sorts of infractions—in some employee personnel files. When asked if she thought these were an effective management tool, Melinda stated, "These people don't have good intentions in their hearts, and that must be documented." Sam had no idea what that meant, and his question, therefore, went unanswered.

- While some Vunorri personnel files had the aforementioned warning paperwork, most did not contain official performance appraisals. Some employees had not been officially reviewed in five years, and that normally meant they had also not received raises.

- Sam had to ask about one particular incident— a sexual harassment complaint filed by a female warehouse worker. Melinda revealed that they settled with the employee before firing her two weeks later for being 10 minutes late to work. He jotted down in his notebook Melinda's sage advice for the now-ex-employee: "Quit wearing tight jeans in a warehouse, and this kind of thing won't happen to you, sweetie."

- When asked about hiring criteria, Melinda really let loose. She was openly hostile toward gay candidates ("an immoral aberration," as she described it), veterans ("a little too battered to be able to come in and think straight") and African-Americans ("blacks don't work as hard").

- Sam asked about The Notebook, and Melinda steadfastly refused to answer any questions about it. The mere mention of The Notebook infuriated her, she denied Sam access to it, and she demanded to know who told him about its existence. Sam declined to say.

We now return you to your regularly scheduled uncomfortable interview, already in progress.

"These three terminations two years ago," Sam said. "A few managers were let go...the paperwork doesn't lay out a reason. Why were these people terminated?"

"Sometimes you have to cut off some heads if you want to be taken seriously."

"Cut off heads?" Sam asked.

"You heard me."

"Melinda, I appreciate a well-run business as much as the next guy, and I know Vunorri has its share of challenges, but some of your policies, I have to say, are a little blunt."

"And?"

"Well," Sam replied, "if you're ranking instruments, I'd say precision ranks above blunt."

"You'd be wrong," Melinda shot back. "I can get people to do what I want them to do. If that's pipe down, they pipe down. If that's quit, they often resign. You can desire results all day. *I get results.*"

Sam prayed at the altar of results, but for some reason, he was dissatisfied with her response.

"Melinda, there's more than one way to skin a cat. Some of this actually sounds illegal. As a leader of this organization, why do you feel it necessary to strong-arm people?"

"Because sometimes that's what it takes, my dear," Melinda sneered. "We're a struggling company. You can't have missed that in your little study here. We have too many substandard people working at Vunorri. I'm doing what's necessary to keep the ship afloat."

How strange—Sam was instinctively dissatisfied with that answer, as well. It was a pro-business sentiment, which jibed with his sensibilities, but he was feeling an odd rush of emotions—feeling *bad* for the Vunorri employees who had to deal with this monster. He had no time to analyze his feelings or understand where this empathy was coming from. Melinda was staring a fiery hole right through him.

"Shouldn't an HR department serve its citizens?" Sam asked. "Your version of an HR department seems to keep its foot planted squarely on their necks." Melinda's frown could have sufficed for an answer. She was not used to anyone questioning her methods or authority.

She leaned in closer to Sam, so close that Sam could almost smell her breakfast. "I don't have to explain myself to you," she growled. "It's clear you haven't learned much in your short time at Vunorri. Dick said you were the real deal—one of the best. He was wrong. As usual. We're done here."

"We are most certainly not done!" Sam protested. "I have more questions!"

"Well, ask 'em to the wall. You're not getting any more answers from me." And with that, Melinda rose to her feet and walked out of the conference room.

"*Come back here*!" Sam yelled.

Sam deserved a beer.

The day had lived up to its billing. Melinda was a double-dealing, intimidating backbiter—a honey badger, cunning and ruthless, with not a hint of joy in her life. She was so cold, so calculating, so lecherous and tyrannical, that being in her presence took Sam's breath away.

He was displeased with himself that he had lost his composure. A plan to be aggressive turned into a train wreck. At least he had gathered a plethora of interesting information. And found his way to a bar.

He pulled up a barstool and labored to sit down, his head lowered.

"Rough day?" the bartender asked.

"You could say that," Sam responded. "I just got tenderized."

"Woman trouble?"

"You have *no* idea, my friend."

CHAPTER 8

MAKING THE COFFEE

As the fire-breathing unicorn stood watch outside, Melinda labored in the castle kitchen, wearing a purple tutu and making pancakes. Strangely, once the plate got to the cavernous dining hall and Sam's long wooden table, he was staring at two poached eggs with imitation bacon bits sprinkled on top. His ornate dining room throne now had electric chair-style wrist straps, and he was immobilized.

"Now," Melinda said, "when we burn Vunorri to the ground, we can leave no traces of our DNA. No evidence, honey! I'm going for the bearer bonds. You grab as many staplers as you can." Sam wanted to object to this nefarious plan, but his mouth was one thousand pounds heavy, stuck in quicksand, and he couldn't get it to move. Suddenly, a fearsome creature with three Pauly Shore heads and the body of Cerberus was standing before him, smoke shooting out of its six nostrils. Like a crazed bull on a crabby Monday morning, the creature roared with his rusty chainsaw growl and lunged at Sam.

"*Noooooooooo!*" Sam screamed as he bounded out of bed.

"Sam, what's the matter?" his dazed wife asked.

"It had three Pauly Shore heads!" Sam shouted.

"That must've been some dream. You were talking in your sleep. By the way, who is Melinda?" she asked with a hint of jealousy.

Oh dear, Sam thought. Something was oh so wrong. Melinda was now in his nightmares. And Sam never had nightmares.

Sam arrived at Vunorri on pins and needles, too unsettled to be able to calm his mind. This was a "call in sick" day, except for the fact that consultants don't get paid time off. "Go get yourself some coffee," he said to himself.

Not again! The coffee had not yet been made! This was all he needed. Then...it occurred to him. *Make the coffee.* Crazy Charlie had advised him to do so, and his current predicament left him no choice. He stared at what looked to him like a Rube Goldberg contraption. Grinders and settings and tubes and carafes. Where does the water go? He stood still in front of it until it became clear—put the carafe in place and press the green "BREW" button.

Three Vunorri associates then entered the room, looking for their morning fix as well. They filled up and turned to leave before one broke away and approached Sam. "Sam, right? Hey, *thank you* for making the coffee. That's really nice of you. No one ever does it."

"Don't mention it," Sam said. "What's your name again?"

"Shelby, from HR. Have a great day, Sam," she said with a smile as she departed.

Hmmm, that's odd. Feeling just a bit better.

"So, how did yesterday go?" Charlie asked in a caring tone as Sam took a seat at his lunch table.

"Yesterday," Sam said, "was *the* car crash you predicted, and more. I ran into a buzz saw. I've worked with hundreds of upper management types in my career, but no one ever like her. She is a cruel beast, with no pain receptors."

"Beast, Sam?" Charlie muttered.

"She had me completely off balance. I didn't really believe you until I experienced her myself. Except for one HR employee, Melinda and her team seem detached from the rest of the company—untouchable. And Dick doesn't seem to know, or care. The things she's capable of..."

"Untouchable is an apt way to put it," Charlie said. "She's like the mafia—avoid reprisals no matter what!"

Sam said that, based on Charlie's warning, he went in to the Melinda meeting guns blazing, and that the plan didn't work. Moreover, as much as he didn't want to, he admitted to Charlie that the entire experience was uncomfortable for him. Worst of all, he really had no idea what he had gained from the entire day, except a super-weird nightmare that he'd keep to himself.

"She rises above merely unpleasant to the level of menacing," Charlie said. "She puts the company at legal risk, not to mention putting everyone on edge. She's a clear and present danger to Vunorri—someday, it'll come to a head.

"For her, the end justifies the means. If you think about it, she's really nothing more than a bully. No long-term value is being created, but her fortress is secure."

"So what the heck's wrong with her?" Sam asked.

"I know very little of her background. One story floating around is that Dick was trying to hire a true number two, someone to run the whole operation and report directly to him. For some reason, he never made the hire, but Melinda was openly vying for the position and felt slighted that she didn't get it. So now she's pissed, but continues to have Dick's ear. Revenge might be her dish.

"At this point, Sam, there's one thing on everyone's mind. Round four. That next round of layoffs. No one wants to see that day come. So our people are nervous wrecks because they think the slower performance of the company and our managers' worsening attitudes must mean that layoffs are coming again. You know, in two of the three rounds, the employees just kind of disappeared. We didn't even get to say goodbye. They were unceremoniously sacked. That's a great British word for 'fired.' Sacked!"

"Look Charlie, sometimes you have to do layoffs."

"Sam, I don't disagree, but you can do 'em in such a way that the departing employees keep their dignity. Did you hear about the first round of layoffs, with HR drones stripping cubes down and…?"

"I did, yesterday," Sam admitted.

"Take their humanity into consideration, Sam! Try to give them a soft landing! Think about this: every employee is someone's special little son or daughter. Every human being is someone's special someone. People treat their own kids with such white-glove reverence, but have no compunction about treating everyone else like crap. I've never understood that. Why can't an employer treat their employees with at least a muted version of that reverence? I mean, these laid-off people aren't like the trash we take out to the dumpster. *They're human beings!*"

"Charlie, you gotta consider lawsuits and stuff like…"

"Ahhhh, that's baloney. Just treat people with dignity and respect. Plain and simple. It shouldn't be that hard."

"But what does it matter? A job loss is a job loss," Sam said.

"He plunged to his death," Charlie responded.

"What?" Sam cried.

"Or, he died in his sleep. Which is the worse way to go? Either way, Sam, the person is dead—gone forever. It certainly couldn't matter how they died, right? One hundred out of one hundred people would choose a peaceful death in their sleep. But by your definition, it shouldn't matter. Why *does* it matter? People are actually comforted by the idea that a loved one died in their sleep. But if that loved one had been stabbed 10 times and then thrown off the top of a building only to be run over by a steamroller, that would be no worse, right? He suffered beforehand, and it's tragic, but it's no worse, correct? Of course it's worse! We know this. Humans have the ability to cogitate on such a situation and come to an appropriate conclusion. We effortlessly apply this thinking to the end of life. Why don't we apply it in life, at work?"

"Because it doesn't help a company hit its numbers," Sam said.

"There are countless ways to be lazy about how you treat people," Charlie continued. "It's much harder to consider the feelings of others and treat them nicely. We could treat each other better at work—why not? *And*, if you want to look at it in a transactional way, what can be bought with this? Happier, more productive employees."

"Alright, listen," Sam said, "tomorrow I have four interviews, and you're lucky to be first. Busy day. We'll get started around 8:15 a.m., OK?"

"Think about what I said, Sam. Take special note of how Melinda made you feel. Think about what this did to both your psyche, *and* your productivity. I gotta get back to the mailroom. I'll see you tomorrow morning."

Upon Charlie's departure, Sam immediately considered what he had heard. Yes, he was mentally under the weather—no doubt about that. Melinda had his number. And true, he had accomplished very little with her.

He wondered, though, if all of this Vunorri turmoil and heartache was just a function of the layoffs themselves. Downsizing is a tough time for any company, no matter what. And without question, one of the tools in his fix-it toolbox was layoffs. Sam had seen this time and again: companies put off making the hard decisions until they're top-heavy. Or market conditions shift and suddenly they're way overstaffed. Sometimes organizations have to reduce headcount, and it's never easy.

What was Charlie saying about layoffs? Be nice? "Really sorry we canned you. You'll find another job real quick. Hope things turn out OK." Why would anyone want to hear that? Sam didn't have an answer, but to him, it was a surprise he was considering an answer to the question in the first place.

CHAPTER 9

CHARLIE'S TRIBUNAL

"IF YOU DON'T MIND, CHARLIE, LET'S GET STARTED IMMEDIATELY."

Charlie took a seat in Sam's assigned office and got comfortable. Part of Sam's promise to Dick was to interview everyone at the company. So this had to include Charlie. Some of the interviews, like the ones with warehouse and factory personnel, would last as little as five or ten minutes. Sam had dined with Charlie enough to know that he needed to book a solid half hour.

"I only have five or so questions for you," Sam said, "and I'll have you on your way."

"How long do we have together?" Charlie ominously asked.

"It shouldn't take that long. I'll have to get to my next meeting pretty quickly. You may or may not, from your position in the mailroom, be able to help me. But I'm obliged to interview you."

"Well Sam, I just can't thank you enough," Charlie said with his salty wit.

"First question for you: We're looking to improve processes here at Vunorri. Can you share with me some ideas you might have?"

"Sam, I'm sure this fact hasn't been lost on you, but there's a lot of negativity flowing through this place. Why is that a problem? Because negativity can take root in and gain control of even the strongest, most positive person. It's stunting the growth of our employees and our company. The broken process I'm talking about is the way we treat each other.

"There was recently an interview with Billy Joel in *The New York Times*. They asked him about his negative reviews." Charlie reached for a newspaper he had brought to the meeting. "Keep in mind, this is the superstar, Billy Joel. The interviewer asked, 'Over the years you talked a lot about being angry, about how critics responded to you and would even on occasion read and rip up bad reviews on stage.' You know what Mr. Joel said? 'That never went away. I read things, and I didn't think they were fair or true. *I would get my back up.* There could be seven other very good reviews, but I only paid attention to the bad ones.' Sam, we're talking about Billy Joel here! He's a beloved American icon. How could he not handle the occasional negative review? To quote you, Sam, why should he care? Didn't he just know he was awesome? Wasn't his whole career proof of that? Couldn't he take solace in his piles of money and his ability to attract women like Christie Brinkley?"

"Maybe he should have," Sam responded.

"No, Sam. Not possible. It's not how we're wired. Negativity is an insipid force, next to impossible to shake off or ignore. Even a tiny dose of it can grab a hold of you and not let go. Why must our employees spend their cranial free cycles trying to overcome Vunorri Inc.'s negativity? Shouldn't they be working on improving our processes? So, the first process that needs improving is no process at all—it's the elimination of a systemic problem that's wrapped around our necks, but needs to let go. We have to find a way to bring some more positivity to this workplace."

Sam didn't consider that to be much of an answer, but he didn't have time to dicker over it.

"Charlie, what problems have you encountered here that management might not know about?"

"We have a huge issue here at Vunorri, and it's our management team. Their approach to managing people needs an overhaul. Human Resources is the most glaring example, but we have this problem in most every corner of the organization.

"This is Human Relations 101. People don't like to be told what to do. They don't like to be beaten down and forced to believe things they don't truly believe. That's why it's so difficult to defeat an insurgency. You can overpower your opponents, but you haven't captured their hearts. You can stomp on them, keep their necks under your foot, but you'll never change the way they feel, except perhaps to further anger them. Beating and defeating them doesn't change their beliefs, and they'll *never* forget that you tried to beat them.

"Vunorri's managers do an abysmal job of convincing their employees that what they're asking them to do is a good idea *and* in their best interests. They don't care to even make this case. Huge mistake."

Charlie had previously proven to be an intelligent man, if not a little eccentric, so Sam was looking for more. But he wasn't getting what he wanted yet. After a bit of back and forth, Sam again went limp and just accepted the answer.

"Next question. What does management do well here at Vunorri?"

"That's easy," Charlie said. "They manage by the seat of their pants, with little concern for the lives and careers of the people they're managing."

"That's not saying much," Sam shot back. "Give me an example."

"They manage people based on whether they like them or not, based on the strength of the little kingdoms they've constructed for themselves here, based on societal prejudices, you name it. You've caught on to this already, right, Sam? I'm sure you've heard the business credo, 'You can't manage what you can't measure.' Well our managers take no measurements—no stock in their people. Worst of all, they don't seem to care about the plight of the folks working for them.

"Humans make assumptions on thin information all too often, and our managers are no different. An old saying goes, 'Everyone you meet is waging a battle about which you know nothing.' That alone should get our managers thinking differently, but it's no use. They just assume that their employees don't care. They have no idea what their employees are going through outside of work. They consider them to be replaceable parts, cogs in the wheel. Probably not the answer you were looking for."

No kidding. This was growing tiresome for the interrogator.

"What could management do better? And Charlie, can we please keep it brief?"

"I am not a terse man. OK, Sam, I'll lay it out for you. Do you know what Vunorri employees really want?"

"A raise?" Sam guessed.

"Maybe. That might be what they think they want, but it's not what they need. It's not what makes them happy. No, they want to fulfill their human needs.

"Have you heard of Tony Robbins?" Charlie asked.

"Yes, motivational speaker guy," Sam responded. "Why are we talking about Tony Robbins?"

"I'm not a big fan of motivational speakers, but here's one piece of brilliant work of his. He posited the theory that there are six basic human needs we all share. And whether we realize it or not, we're constantly striving to have these needs fulfilled.

"The human needs I'm talking about are comfort, variety, significance, connection, growth, and contribution. When these needs go unmet, we humans don't handle that too well. So consider each. Right now, no Vunorri employee is feeling comfort or certainty, as pretty much everyone knows we're in trouble. There have been layoffs, and we dread round four. We're all feeling very restless. Next, managers like Neil don't challenge their promising employees like Josie—he practically keeps her in a cage, when he's not launching telephony at her. She just came on board a few months ago, and is not only scared and traumatized, but probably bored stiff—no variety.

"Then, managers rarely thank their employees, and like I said, don't give them enough responsibility. I won't name names, but did you know there's a department here at Vunorri that plays a very special drinking game?"

"A drinking game?" Sam asked.

"Yes. The head of the department thanks his or her employees so infrequently that, when it does happen, whichever employee was thanked has to take the whole department out drinking. Funny, but sad. Most here don't feel a sense of significance. Their work doesn't engender such a feeling.

"The next human need—connection, or love. Some people like making friends at work, some don't. Here, there are pockets of friends, but most people at Vunorri are just tired of each other. The fifth human need goes spectacularly unmet—no raises, not many promotions, not learning many new skills, lots of burnout. So no growth. And contribution? Forget about it. So, for the most part, Vunorri employees are failing miserably at fulfilling their six basic human needs. This causes and exacerbates our unhappiness.

"Sam, have you heard of Seth Godin?"

"Yes, wrote *Purple Cow*?" Sam impatiently responded.

"In one of his best books, *Linchpin*, he wrote, 'Dignity is more important than wealth. Given a choice between dignity and wealth, most people choose dignity. Respect matters.' I think that's brilliant. I think we as humans think we want more stuff, but what makes us feel really great about ourselves is dignity. Was 'wealth' in Robbins' six human needs? It was not.

"So we want our own human needs fulfilled. That's what makes one's life complete. Here's the trick, Sam—the act of fulfilling the human needs of *others* fulfills our own. Such selfless acts can turn incivility into civility, inaction into action, lack of productivity into productivity. The active effort of fulfilling the human needs of others can cause these great things to happen. So when I..."

"Charlie, I'm going to have to stop you. You didn't answer my question. I said..."

"I most certainly did answer your question. Management needs to do a better job of supporting their people and helping them fulfill their human needs. That would almost assuredly reduce our turnover rate, right?"

Sam wanted none of it. "*Why* are we talking about Tony Robbins and Seth Godin? What does this have to do with saving money and profits and avoiding a fourth round of layoffs?"

"More than you care to know, Sam."

"I want to steer this ship back to center," Sam said. "Charlie, have you ever come across any cost-saving ideas you'd like to share with me?"

"Sam, let me ask *you*: will it matter if we save some money here and there if none of us can even get along? Who cares about money if we can't work as a team and respect each other with a minimum amount of human decency?

"Everyone gets a label here at Vunorri, and it's a huge problem. 'I'm management, and you're an entry-level grunt. I'm a hard-working white guy, and you're one of the lazy black workers.' No one deserves to be pigeonholed like that."

"Charlie..." Sam interrupted. But Charlie didn't even hear him, and didn't stop pontificating.

"When observing that a person is black or white, gay or straight, whatever...what do you think you know about them? Ask yourself, Sam: why do we immediately search for a slot in the accordion folder in which to place people?

"Often, when we notice such differences and they don't conform to our vision of the world, we give that person no quarter. Note that, in many circumstances, they're quite used to this. Black people have always been black, Michael Jackson notwithstanding. When you label someone 'black' and then mistreat them, you're not the first person to do so. A lifetime of perceiving situations means they notice that you notice this about them, and their alarms and defense systems immediately turn on.

"When you label someone, you knock them right off their feet and give them no chance, which is no way to start a friendship or working relationship.

"So Sam, the real reason we don't get along is because *we are* different. We're all so different here, and we *always* notice that about each other, and we almost always let it divide us. We work with fellow employees who are hard-driving, shy, meek, outspoken, conservative, liberal, gay, straight, black, white, Jewish, and I could go on.

"Our asymmetries are wedges we place between ourselves, or the wedges are strategically and nefariously placed there for us. We find it difficult to relate to others, to be friends with them, to be cordial enough to even speak to them, and ultimately, it's a challenge to work with them. Workers on the factory line don't want to commiserate with the wealthy owners. The rank and file don't trust them. The wealthy owners often think less of their workers. After all, they haven't accomplished as much in life, have they? We often hear the phrase 'Diversity is our strength.' Is that always so? No matter the answer, we have a great challenge before us. If diversity in talent, race, religion and social strata is leaving us divided and working in isolation, what can we do?"

"Come on, Charlie, I don't know! This is all great, but I have questions for you, and I need your answers. These soliloquies on human nature are not what I'm looking for."

Charlie did not seem to care. "Well I don't wanna talk about margins and headcounts and processes and profits. You need to learn about a completely different set of tactics. Managing human beings!"

Sam was getting severely, stabbingly, groin-grabbingly agitated. "But that doesn't answer my..."

Charlie continued like a runaway freight train. More and more, story after story. If this interview had been an R&B song, it would be, "On and On, To the Break of Dawn." He wasn't even taking breaths as he launched into one topic after the other, all revolving around human relations. Charlie reminded Sam of his own grandpa, who would never shut up about "back in my day..." Finally, Charlie made an observation about his unwilling interlocutor.

"This all seems a bit lost on you, Sam."

"I'm not lost!" Sam cried. "I'm here with a specific set of questions, and you're not even *trying* to answer them! Charlie, what in Sam Hill is wrong with you? I didn't schedule this interview to have you recite a Dale Carnegie book to me!"

"You're right!" Charlie exclaimed. "This *is* Dale Carnegie stuff! Maxims to live by, a deep dive on what motivates people, a blueprint for how to treat each other, first proffered by the man in a book published in 1936! Nineteen thirty-six! It's almost shameful we still have to discuss these things. Maybe you think it sounds a little too self-help-ey and it's apparently turning you off. But *we need help*! Vunorri Inc., the human race, and the tribes of said humans working at businesses everywhere desperately need help!

"Getting people to think this way is a huge change. Maybe too big. Can we really pull together at the same table the richest, most stubborn owners, and the laziest, most stubborn workers who don't trust their bosses, and force them to have a sit-down? Can we coax them into understanding each other better? Can we ask them to consider the human needs of each other? This might be too much to ask.

"However, we have to try. Throughout history, the activist heroes who've demanded change in our world have been very stubborn people, employing a range of annoying tactics. These range from violence to polemics to sit-in protests to simply outlasting their opponents."

Sam was unmoved, and didn't even realize *he* had just been outlasted. "Who cares? I don't need a veritable congressional filibuster from you. I have to ... oh my God, it's noontime??? I've blown through my next two meetings!" Charlie seemed to find that mildly humorous.

"I'm afraid you still don't understand people, Sam—what makes 'em tick, what motivates them. Shouldn't a consultant like you, responsible for getting the right people on the right seats on the bus at the companies you consult for—a guy responsible for making lay-offs—shouldn't a guy like you have mastered the finer art of human relations?"

Without another word, Sam gathered his papers and bolted out of the room. While frazzled and hustling to where his next meeting was to have taken place hours previously, he thought of Charlie and said to himself, "Geez, does this guy ever shut up?"

The answer was irretrievably no, and that seemed to suit Charlie just fine.

CHAPTER 10

CRUELTY AT WORK

FOR SAM, THE END OF WEEK TWO AT VUNORRI COULD NOT HAVE come soon enough. He had never been much of a clock watcher, but to assess his current situation would have him admit that he wasn't making much progress and wasn't having much fun. He had a pounding headache. Stress was in control—he was down in the dumps.

Today would be spent out in the warehouse, finally conducting interviews with the warehouse manager Rod and his personnel. For his interview, Rod was hosting Sam at his desk, a ramshackle wooden table near the dock doors. After about 45 minutes of interview questions, Sam heard a commotion whose sound rose above the normal white noise of conveyor belts, boxes, and packing tape. He heard shouting, and when he looked over, he saw a crowd gathered.

Rod rose to attend to the situation, but then something odd happened. Sam bounded to his feet and moved even more quickly than Rod. If you asked Sam what had been going through his mind, to this day he probably wouldn't be able to tell you. Instinctually, he ran over to the crowd and found two employees engaged in a fight. A few fists were thrown before the two grabbed each other and wrestled. They fell to the ground and started barrel rolling across the floor, over and

over like a bad NASCAR accident. Sam grabbed one of the partici-
pants and pulled him off his opponent before screaming, "Hey guys,
break it up! *Stop!* That's enough! Get back to work!"

After a bit, the crowd dispersed, and Rod prepared to find out
what happened and document the situation. A rather inauspicious
start to another day at Vunorri.

"Thanks, Sam," Rod said. "I appreciate you lending a hand. What
got into you?"

"I don't know. Those two shoulda been working, not fighting."

After the altercation, Sam hit the washroom to clean up. He
would continue with Rod and his team later. Right now, he needed
to calm his head and compose himself. He splashed water on his face
and looked in the cloudy bathroom mirror. What *had* gotten into
him? Why was he jumping into a brawl with two crazed warehouse
workers? He had given Rod a very corporate answer, but the nagging
truth was that he really didn't know why he had played "hero."

On the walk back to his office, a familiar face stopped him in
the hallway.

"Hi, Sam."

"Hi, Shelby. What's going on?"

"I don't have time to talk," she said quietly. "Here," and she handed
Sam a sheet of paper.

"What's this?" Sam asked.

"I know you're working hard to try to help Vunorri. I wanted you
to see this. I just can't take it anymore."

"What am I supposed to..."

"Just read it," Shelby interrupted. "Help change this place." And with that, she walked away.

The sheet of paper was a printout of an e-mail exchange between Shelby and her boss Melinda. Sam scanned the page. Shelby started by requesting that Melinda quit insulting her day after day. Apparently Melinda didn't think much of the college Shelby attended, nor the quality of the work she was providing Vunorri. Shelby had tried to ignore the constant barbs, but her pride finally got the best of her, and she asked that Melinda cool it.

Unfortunately, this was something that Shelby was just going to have to put up with, because Melinda unleashed the mother of all polemics, writing back to her:

You're making too many mistakes. That much is clear. Do thorough, excellent, error-free work, and we won't have a problem and I won't ever feel compelled to knock your degree. Perhaps do the kind of work that would honor your pedigree. Speaking of that, I've half-considered verifying that you actually got a degree from that fancy university of yours. But you're right, I should only have questioned the integrity of the final product and left out the insults. Maybe instead of being petulant, defensive and brooding, you'd be better served by embracing contrition, humility, and a laser-focused attention to detail and professionalism.

You're quite green on how the business world functions. You have much work to do to impress me, and you waste your time sending worthless notes like this? I suggest you learn to play nice with the sharks if you want to cut it at Vunorri. Otherwise, you're going to be a failure

*here and everywhere you go in life. You shouldn't forget
that I'm your boss. I could mess up your life big-time if
I needed to. If this job isn't for you, there are other companies in town. Oh wait—no other HR department
would think of taking you on.*

*I've enjoyed educating you on your place in this food
chain. You're welcome. Never write an e-mail like this
to me again.*

Sam was aghast at what he was reading. The first word that came
to mind was *despicable*. Utterly so. A cascading series of ugly feelings began falling over him, swarming around his head, sticking to
him. All of this negativity and offensiveness—sadistic head games,
fistfights!—was starting to accumulate like plaque on teeth, just as
Charlie said it would.

"Sam, you look like you've seen a ghost," Charlie said as he came
into the lunchroom. "May I sit with you?" Sam just stared at the piece
of paper in his hands, saying nothing.

"Sam?"

"I just don't understand this...this *behavior*," Sam said as he gestured
toward the e-mail he was holding. "Why would someone act like this?"

"What do you have there?" Charlie asked.

"Here, read this."

Charlie read the e-mails between Shelby and Melinda. "Wow.
Everyone knows Melinda is a tough customer, but that's really something. You probably shouldn't have shown that to me."

"At this point, what's the difference?"

"How did reading that make you feel?" Charlie asked.

"Pretty crappy," Sam said. "It's disgusting. And I'm surprised I feel this way. Little incidents like this happen at every organization. Why is this bothering me?"

Sam paused, and quickly came to a realization—he had never been this honest with Charlie before. He was almost proud of himself. But he then realized that was an incorrect deduction. He had been honest with Charlie from day one, but something was different now. Him. He was changing.

"Sam, can I ask you a question? *Why* do you do what you do?"

"Oh, not again..."

"Just answer the question, Sam."

"I have a family to raise, and..."

"No, Sam. Why do you work the job that you work?"

"I guess I've never thought about it."

"You've never asked yourself, 'Why am I here?' Some people believe we were put here on Earth for a reason. I've sat at a desk, at a job that was dragging me down, thinking, 'This just *can't* be why we're here on this planet. Two weeks of vacation means you spend 50 weeks working? I'm *here?* Doing *this?* Working with *them?* Putting up with *that?*' There's no way this can be part of anyone's master plan."

"I guess I'm just not a deep thinker like you," Sam said.

"Oh nonsense, you've probably thought about this stuff and didn't even realize it. I question my purpose in life all of the time. My purpose, at least currently, is to become a better person every day. Not a richer person, but a wiser person. I don't identify with my job, per se, but in my capacity here, I try to make great things happen."

"Why are you asking me about my life's purpose?" Sam asked.

"One of our strengths as human beings, when we choose to embrace it, is our propensity for inquiry. When kids interminably ask "Why? Why, mom? Why, dad? Why? Why? *Why*?" they're searching for answers—for understanding. Why don't adults like us ask "why" anymore? Do we think we have the whole world sussed out? We already have all the answers? If we did, Sam, you'd have this place printing money by now.

"All of life's greatest mysteries and challenges, from the origin of the universe to the cure for polio, all the way down to 'Why the heck is Melinda still employed here?' come down to a question of 'Why?' Things don't get better unless we ask, 'Why?' And if no one else is asking why, *someone needs to*," Charlie said, lightly striking the table with his fist.

"So I ask you. Why do we choose to treat each other so poorly here at Vunorri? Why were those two guys fighting instead of devising ways to pack more shipments per hour? Why does Melinda choose to insult her own employees? Don't you want to know why?"

"Well," Sam responded, "would it help me change Vunorri's fortunes for the better?"

"*Yes*!!! Melinda and Neil would shape up or ship out. Dick would be a hands-on owner and show some human compassion for his employees. Everyone here would work their tails off. Of course it would help!

"Sam, the best workplace is one in which none of this silliness happens. No horrible e-mails, no backstabbing, no politics, no cruelty, and for goodness sakes, no fistfights! So yes, put me on record as being in favor of a kinder, happier workplace."

Sam walked into the foyer of his home and threw his keys onto the tray near the front door. It was 9:00 p.m., and he was ready for dinner and some night paperwork. His wife immediately appeared from the kitchen.

"Where have you been? I've been calling you. Texting you. You missed Jaime's soccer game. *Again*. She was incredibly upset."

Sam looked down at the floor, not feeling like facing his wife. His work schedule usually prevented him from attending his daughter's activities, so they should have been used to his absence by now. Sure, in a perfect world, he'd attend all family events. But who would get all of this important company-saving work done?

"Time just got away from me. I didn't see it on my calendar. This engagement is a tough one."

"What has gotten into you lately?" she asked with increasing emphasis. "You're talking in your sleep about women named Melinda. You're gone all the time and a pill when you're around. You're not even trying to be a father. I feel like a single mom here."

What *had* gotten into him? He was stressed, and felt like he was coming unglued, slowly but surely. Oddly, he was experiencing guilt for having missed the soccer game. And that last pipe bomb line of hers really burned him. He cared about his daughter, and felt like he pitched in around the house (even though he was wrong).

"What's the matter with you? Why don't you want to come watch your own daughter play soccer?"

"I'm busy."

His wife wore exasperation all over her weary face. "Who are you becoming, Sam? Ask yourself if it's all really worth it."

Upon that little piece of advice, she went off to bed, and Sam got sick to his stomach. Dinner would be self-canceled. His family had dealt with "busy Sam" in the past. What was so different this time? He lay on the couch, thinking he could doze off watching TV. But it was no use. He was exhausted and wide awake. As much as he tried, he could not turn off the spinning turbine of his mind. All he could think about was Vunorri, that fight, Melinda, the bank...and Charlie. He felt a slight tinge of remorse over how dismissively he had been treating Charlie.

And then, it happened. Sam began talking to himself aloud, without the self-awareness that this was a really bad sign. "Maybe the workplace *can* be transformed. Maybe people can be taught work manners. Maybe they *need* to be." A feeling of dread came over him. "Wow, is the old man onto something?"

PART THREE

RESPECT FOR BUSINESS GOAL NO.1: HAPPINESS

"Emotion is the force of life."
—TONY ROBBINS

"Trying to be happy by accumulating possessions is like trying to satisfy hunger by taping sandwiches all over your body."
—GEORGE CARLIN

"Seize the time—live now! Make now always the most precious time. Now will never come again!"
—CAPTAIN JEAN-LUC PICARD, *Star Trek* TNG episode "The Inner Light"

CHAPTER 11

A 100,000-HOUR WORK LIFE

This was the first Monday morning Vunorri management meeting Sam had attended. On the docket were the usual departmental reports, mostly droning on and on about things that had already happened or problems that somebody needed to solve. Then, a cold bucket of water was thrown on the proceedings.

"What is *he* doing here?" Neil asked as he pointed in the direction of Sam.

"I thought his attendance would be a good learning exercise for him," Dick said. "And I wanted him to report on his findings so far."

"Well, I'll be frank," Neil said. "I don't need some hot shot outside guy who knows nothing about Vunorri telling me how to do my job. And his presence has been beyond disruptive to my department."

Sam should have been used to such Vunorri face slaps by now, but he wasn't. "Neil, I was with your department for two days before you..."

"I have to agree with Neil," Melinda interrupted. "This exercise seems like it's going nowhere. He comes in totally unprepared. We don't have time to waste on some wild goose chase put on by an amateur."

"Hold on a minute!" Sam angrily said.

"You have no idea what you're doing," Neil said.

"Are you new at this line of work?" Melinda asked sarcastically.

"Guys, guys," Dick said, as he gestured to Sam, Neil, and Melinda to settle down. "He's here at Vunorri until his work is done. I need all of you to help him out. Understood?"

That would be the last Monday morning meeting Sam would attend.

Sam walked out of the meeting and headed to his office. It would be clichéd to say that he had never been so embarrassed in all his life, but that felt about right. Bruised pride—the big, ugly purple bruise kind. Totally humiliating to be dressed down like that in front of the entire management team. What a vulgar display by Neil and Melinda—so demeaning and despicable that Sam was feeling waves of anger and disgust. He was dreaming up comeback after witty comeback that he *should* have delivered to them when he had the chance. So many good zingers! Revenge was on his mind—what could he do to get back at these contemptible people?

Then he hit "pause" on those thoughts and tried to take a deep breath. Revenge? This was not who Sam was. Why was his mind even going there? Well, because he was pissed! Yesterday's warehouse fight, the horrible Melinda e-mail, being an absentee dad and upsetting his family, all of Charlie's awful stories, and now this? The plaque was getting worse, the events disfiguring what was normally a very composed spirit and intellect.

Sam tried to get his world spinning on its axis again. "What does any of this have to do with saving Vunorri?" he asked himself. He needed to sort through it all, and in a cruel, ironic twist of fate, he *sought Charlie out* for lunch. At this bleak juncture, Charlie was the one person who would listen. "What a revolting development," Sam muttered to himself.

Sam spied Charlie in a corner of the lunchroom, alone. "Hey, mind if I bend your ear?" Sam asked.

"Not at all, Sam! Please sit."

Sam proceeded to fill Charlie in on the vagaries of the morning's proceedings. A blow-by-blow account of the meeting—his feelings of wanting to stab Melinda and Neil in the eyes with a pen, and more. Charlie was a good listener.

"I'm glad you didn't snap in the meeting," Charlie said. "I know you wanted to let them have it, but you have a job to do. Tearing them a new one would've released some excellent endorphins, but you'd be no closer to solving the puzzle of Vunorri."

"I just don't understand those two. Why do they act like that?" Sam asked.

"Well, besides the fact they're jerks, I think they lack purpose. Vunorri Inc. is rudderless, and so are they. No direction. It doesn't mean Neil and Melinda *would* fit in if Dick provided them direction.

"But if you don't have purpose, you're totally lost. Remember when we talked about purpose on Friday?"

"Oh heaven forbid, how could I forget?" Sam sarcastically said.

"Well, what's our purpose at work? Do we need one? I think we do. Did you know you'll spend, on average, 100,000 hours of your life at work?

"No, of course I didn't know that."

"Depending on overtime, we're talking about 40-50 years of your life, five days a week. That's a large chunk of time, wouldn't you say? And that comes out of the approximately 250,000 waking hours we'll have as adults. Of course, don't forget that during those 150,000 hours of so-called 'free time,' you'll often be commuting to and from your job, worrying about your job, or going to your job to work overtime. I'm obsessed with that 100,000-hour bucket of work time. It's worth talking about!"

"OK, fine, let's talk about it," Sam said.

"Our work lives have to get better. What a waste of a life, spending time detesting the 100,000 hours. You know, Sam, most people don't like their jobs. All they think about is Powerball lottery tickets and retirement. When planning a vacation, we never obsess about the end. When we get married, we never obsess about the end. When we work, we obsess about the end. What's up with that?"

Sam pursed his lips, thinking of what to say. "Maybe people need to be taught how to care about those working hours," he said. "Maybe they need to be taught *why* to care."

"Wow, Sam. Good! We send our kids to expensive business schools to learn about cost accounting, just-in-time inventory systems, marketing, economics, probability and statistics, business law, information systems, you name it! But we don't spend any time teaching them about human relations? We never teach people how to treat the receptionist? Why *isn't* Dale Carnegie required reading in business school? Why aren't there classes built around making those 100,000 hours a happy, fulfilling time? Oh no, for that, you're on your own!

"We never spend time in business school debating the best way to build human teams—teams that can be both profitable *and* happy. No classes explore this simple fact: vastly different human beings are forced to work together when they join a company. It's a combustible mix of races, levels of ambition, political beliefs, talent levels—everything that makes us different!"

"You think that's why we don't get along?" Sam asked.

"History has shown it's very easy to hate those different than us. We fight wars with those different than us. We really never learn how to look past these intrinsic differences and get along. We never got the training that said, 'Just realize you're going to be working with people not like you. In order to excel, you must look past this.' You can't have kindness and happiness without this understanding.

"Sam, you and me will never be the same, and we may never share the exact same values and beliefs. We need to look past and not worry about our differences. You might think the best teams are made up of talented people with complementary skills. And I agree we can't discount skill, but personality fit is even more important, and then even more important than that, everyone must buy into this idea: we are all different! Accept, respect, move on, and conquer!

"Sam, human beings are not rational creatures. *That's* the construct we must work from."

"Are you going to let me talk?" Sam asked.

"Now that you're making a little sense, I'll consider it," Charlie said with a grin.

Sam was ever so slightly continuing to bend. He was allowing his mind to consider the possibilities of Charlie's point of view. "How do you suppose we can teach people to look past these so-called 'intrinsic differences' and care about each other?" Sam asked.

Charlie did not hesitate to answer. "We lack the perspective to care about each other. That has to change."

"What kind of perspective?"

"Hmmm, how can I best explain this? Have you ever seen the news stories about some random group of people stuck in an elevator together for a long time? It usually goes like this: after eight hours trapped, the air is getting thick and fetid. The cellphone batteries have perilously dropped into the single digits. Those trapped are scared, hungry, and thirsty, and they really have to pee. With little to do other than panic or chat, they begin talking about their jobs, families, hobbies, ways to escape, and the first thing they're going to do when they're finally rescued.

"They didn't know each other before their ordeal, and they're almost certainly from different walks of life, but now they've bonded. What could cause such a bond to occur?"

"Well, they were trapped," Sam said. "All they could do was talk to each other."

"Exactly. Each captive got to know someone they would've never found time or reason to befriend, and they did so in a deeply profound way. They might even exchange phone numbers and stay in contact. They now respect each other because of what they've been through together and it doesn't matter if it was a disparate mix of CEOs, janitors, Jews, blacks, gay people, whatever.

"To survive, they came to an understanding. They set aside their differences in pursuit of three common goals: passing the time, not going crazy, and survival.

"The employees of Vunorri need to set aside their differences in pursuit of three business goals—better teamwork, more profits, and above all, happiness. To convince our people to set aside their differences, to give them that perspective they lack, we have to somehow get them to take a walk in each other's shoes."

"Well," Sam said, "it doesn't seem like we can entrap people in an elevator to achieve the desired result. That's not a sustainable business practice." Charlie let out a lighthearted laugh, and Sam couldn't help himself either.

"Charlie, can I ask you a question? Why is this stuff so important to you?"

"Simple: I would rather see people happy, instead of frustrated, unfulfilled, and sad. Wouldn't you?"

"I don't know...I don't know what to think now. When I pull the triggers that need pulling in order to improve companies, happiness isn't one of my concerns. I've always thought, 'you're either a happy person or you're not.' My role as a consultant never seemed to be one of happiness cultivation. You know what I mean? There's a job to be done."

"Well," Charlie responded, "I've always noticed that CEOs and upper management respond to value propositions. So, know this: there *is* value in cultivating kindness. Stronger teams are the result. Companies everywhere are desperately trying to build better teams, because that's what management books tell them to do. But they overlook the most important tactic of all.

"Why is happiness and a mindset of kindness and cooperation so important? Think of it this way. In a decade or two, when we all get our neural implants installed, thereby relegating Google Glass to the trash heap, never mind our long-deceased iPhones, the key to our successful use of the technology will *not* be mastering the technology. No, nothing will be more determining and necessary than depositing the right thoughts into the device. Does that make sense Sam?"

"Neural implants? No. That doesn't make sense."

Charlie continued. "If you're trying to learn baseball, you don't master the bat. It's just a piece of wood. You master your preparation, your knowledge of the pitches thrown, and your swing.

"People—and in this case I mean our coworkers—are no different. The first and most important 'tactic' we need to master—the foundation of building great businesses and achieving everything we want in life—are you ready for this, Sam???—is to learn to be nicer to each other! This place needs more nice. Kindness yields happiness. Get it?"

"Well, kindness *is* in short supply around here," Sam said, shrugging his shoulders. "And I hate to admit it to you, but more than a few people around here seem to be unhappy. No one at Vunorri got that teamwork training you talked about. I still don't know how recognizing this fact saves the company, but…"

Sam paused, almost hoping Charlie would jump in as usual and launch into another speech about this or that. But Charlie sat silently, eating his sandwich. Sam had heard Charlie talk about kindness and happiness so much—painfully and redundantly so—and Sam could not deny the simple truth that Vunorri was a gross, unhappy group of people, through and through. At that moment, he felt marginally sorry for Charlie. The old man deserved better than to be stuck in a job at this place.

"Man, how have you lasted here so long?" Sam asked Charlie with a slight chuckle. "I've been here two weeks and I'm pulling my hair out."

Charlie waited for five seconds before confidently stating, "My work here is not done."

CHAPTER 12

THE PRESSURE IS ON

"Sam, can I see you?"

Sam hadn't arrived but two minutes earlier, but it was apparent that Dick needed him now.

"The bank called," Dick said. "They want a progress report. I promised them a plan in 30 days, but they're anxious for an update. What have you found so far?"

The situation was dire. Vunorri was cash-poor, and little did Dick know it, but Sam was answers-poor. Interviews, observations, and Charlie had provided Sam a bunch of nice case study material—great nuggets of advice that could improve most companies—but Vunorri's big problem wasn't theoretical. It was TNT with the fuse lit. The bank was here and now—Vunorri's grim reaper. Sam felt silly for mentally drawing a comparison between the bank and death shrouded in black, but Sam wasn't thinking quite straight right then. His time at Vunorri was bringing him down, slowly transforming him.

"Sam, I need some answers soon. I'm running out of excuses, and now they're telling me they may call the line of credit. The entire balance would immediately become due! I don't have one and a half million dollars to give them! I need the plan."

A lovely start to the day.

"Who are you working with today?" Charlie asked Sam as he sat down to join him for a quick bite.

"I'm out in the warehouse with Rod again. He's such a nice guy. Totally professional—haven't had a single issue with him. Something tells me he doesn't belong here."

"He actually likes it here," Charlie said. "To be honest, he's one of the few. Most people here are tired of management and sick of each other. So jaded, so done with this place. As crazy as it is to say, Dick deserves better."

Now Sam thought he was hallucinating. "Charlie, what's gotten into you? I didn't think you had one ounce of respect for Dick."

"You should know me better by now. I'm fair and even-handed. Business is a two-way street. Sure, 'you-know-what normally rolls downhill,' as they say. But here at Vunorri, it rolls both ways!

"I don't lack respect for Dick, and I wish he wasn't going through this. The vilification of businesspeople like Dick is shortsighted and absurd. Everyone needs a job, right? We need businesses! I'm not elevating the entrepreneur over the worker—you know I wouldn't do that—but we'd do well to understand the importance of the existence of a large network of well-run businesses. And that *has* to include hard-working employees. A worker might say, 'Hey, I'm getting paid. What's the difference?' Employers don't deserve this attitude. But Sam, even more important—such an attitude will never lead to work happiness. And job satisfaction is so low here. Jobs here, and at many companies, are the necessary evil we need in order to feed our families. Retirement, where we'd sit around and do nothing *on purpose*, seems like what we're all steering our boat toward. When all this time, maybe Dick just needed to feel appreciated."

Sam laughed at the notion, but Charlie was unfazed.

"It's true! Employees need to feel a sense of significance. When they're not challenged, when their bosses treat them poorly, they don't feel like they're worth anything. Crazy to think, Sam, but bosses and entrepreneurs feel this way too sometimes."

"If you're so pro-business," Sam protested, "then why all this populist folly? Get out of the way and let Dick run his business."

"*No!* Don't you see? The people who run businesses and the people who work at them are one in the same! They both want to be happy!

"And Sam, I hate to beat a dead horse even deader, but it would be helpful if people around here were nicer to each other."

"Man, you just won't let that go!" Sam exclaimed.

Charlie attentively sat up straight, as if his moment had arrived. He was about to convince Sam once and for all that happiness at work mattered.

"Sam, I have a challenge for you. Can you think of a business situation where happiness—the happiness of employees, from management to worker—would hinder the success of the employee and the organization? Happiness would impede progress, would hold you back and slow you down.

"Do you want a minute to think about it?" Charlie wisecracked.

Sam sat motionless, puzzled. He *really* wanted to bust the old man with one, but he came up empty-handed. Charlie continued.

"OK, try this instead. Can you think of an instance or a business situation where unhappiness could bring on the onset of failure? I need a scenario where unhappiness would slow down, stop progress, or make someone unable to do his or her job.

"You didn't hesitate for a second to think of an example, did you, Sam?"

Sam was uncomfortable when painted into a corner, but that's where he found himself. His next grand statement was painfully clumsy.

"But Charlie, if you're nice in business, competitors will walk all over you. And if the pursuit of happiness run amok causes damage to the organization, that's a huge problem. I mean, what if no one worked hard anymore?"

"Well goodness, be smart about it," Charlie responded. "Being nice and finding happiness doesn't mean 'Thank you sir, may I have another?' We're being nice *to each other*, not giving away competitive secrets. And the pursuit of happiness doesn't mean we drink on the job or work two-day weeks! Always work hard, and be good to your fellow man while doing it."

"But we can't be happy at work all the time," Sam said. "Solving problems and doing great work requires conflict. Can you be happy while slogging your way through a work fight?"

"Happy 100% of the time?" Charlie asked. "No, that seems impossible, and even a little weird. We need to always be pursuing happiness, dealing with the bumps in the road as they present themselves, and most of all, we must respect each other. Disagree without being disagreeable.

"Seriously Sam, get real. No more verbal gymnastics. No more tired, lame, stereotypical corporate fears. I need a *real* example."

While Sam couldn't come up with an answer to Charlie's little challenge, he didn't want to believe Charlie was on to anything substantial. Just didn't want to believe it. And in the back of his mind, he was worrying sick about the bank. And now, the back of his mind was in a fistfight with the front of his mind. It was getting cloudy up there.

"Charlie, what's this fluffy stuff got to do with the numbers?"

Charlie ignored Sam's question. "This would be a huge change in corporate culture, you know? I'm not sure people like you are ready for it."

"You don't know what you're talking about," Sam scoffed.

"You're afraid of this change, because it's big."

Sam's irritation was turning bright red. "Oh baloney. I just question what this does for profits."

"Admit it, Sam. You're not built for this world."

"What's that supposed to mean?"

"This is change you're deathly scared of."

"I'm not afraid of change!" Sam protested.

"No," Charlie responded. "You're afraid of change that affects *you!* You have *no problem* inflicting change on others. You lay people off and throw their lives into turmoil at the drop of a hat! Why is that, Sam? When does the damage end? When you say it ends? When do you stop hurting people? When the pile of money is too tall to even spend? How can you pull the levers of prosperity and destitution like that and experience no remorse? No emotion whatsoever when doing it? Families going hungry because of your decisions. How can you do it, Sam?"

"Because sometimes that's what it takes!" screamed Sam at the top of his lungs, completely unhinged. "You know nothing of business, Charlie! *Nothing*! You've never run a company, have you? Never bore the responsibility of keeping an organization afloat, never mind

prosperous. *Never* had to make tough decisions! You're always talking about people and their happiness. There's a business here that supports hundreds of families! If it doesn't survive and thrive, none of these people will have...*any!*...*money*! So what should we be focusing on again? Happiness???"

"Sam, you may be right, but I'm a happier man than you are."

"Oh you're nuts! You..."

"Wrong," Charlie interrupted in an easy tone. "I *am* happier. And truthfully, I'm the one that knows more about business, because I focus on the human instead of the company. Organizations come and go, Sam. But we remain. We live on to pick up the pieces of our lives. To find meaning and purpose in our daily doings, to work at a dead-end job we hate for our entire adult life so our children can stand on our shoulders and reach for something better, to explain to our wives why we're no longer getting a paycheck, to walk into that first job interview in 20 years feeling worthless and pathetic. We have to live on through all of this, carrying pain around in our hearts, dragging our families through it, hoping to feel worthwhile again, just wanting to find fulfillment and *be happy*. Until our last dying breath, we humans are all that matters. Our happiness and unhappiness—*they alone* are the most important buttons that life presses." Charlie lowered his voice even further, demanding that Sam tune in. "Sam, look at me. The strongest company in the *world* could be created by the management team that understands this."

Sam slowed his panting breaths and tried to settle himself down. Coming unglued as he had was not part of the consulting package he offered. He was embarrassed so many had witnessed it.

Charlie gave Sam a minute, and then continued. "You know how lousy and sad you feel right now? This is the pain that unhappy Vunorri employees feel every day. It's *crushing*, Sam! It's a human horror that more people here don't enjoy their jobs. And it's awful that they take that pain home and exhale it onto their families. And it's a bloody crime, Sam, that those families experience stress because of all of this.

"Sorry to say, but your wife will want nothing to do with you tonight. It's a terrible shame you feel this way right now, my friend."

Sam slumped in his chair, gazing up at the slightly stained ceiling. He was in no shape to do any lucid thinking, and he hated that. As Charlie went about eating his lunch, patiently waiting for Sam to feel like talking again, Sam tried his hardest to consider everything he had heard over the previous two and a half weeks. More importantly, he wondered if there was anything to what Charlie was saying. In the grand scheme of things, did it matter that he felt awful right now? Was this what Charlie wanted him to understand? That his pain today was important to note because it was adversely affecting his performance and psyche, was avoidable, and was therefore simply unacceptable? It seemed plausible to Sam; he didn't want to feel this way anymore.

"Charlie, man, I'm sorry. I'm really sorry I yelled at you."

"Sam, it's OK."

"No, it's not. I think you're right. At this moment in time, you *are* a happier man than I am. Wow." Sam paused for a moment and let out a pained sigh before continuing. "I'm a miserable mess. I can't remember ever feeling this poorly before. My head is ringing...muddled. I can't think right now. I can't even do my job! I'm getting paid huge money to make the big breakthrough here, and I have nothing. My reputation in the industry will be shot!

"I hate coming here, Charlie. I dread this place. Besides you and a few others, everyone is negative here! I'm so screwed up right now. Feeling like this...it's just not worth it. Life's too short."

"For once, my friend, we agree," Charlie said. "Maybe for the first time, come to think of it."

Sam's mind chewed on Charlie's words as he began to refurbish and reconstruct what he knew about business. "Charlie, this is no way to live. I can't imagine a large enough salary to have to deal with all of this. I still have no idea what I'm going to tell Dick, except that Vunorri Inc. is a very special place. *Everything* is wrong!"

Charlie started laughing, which caused Sam to start laughing. Sam needed the levity.

"Charlie, I think I get it now. It's like you said earlier—how can being happy ever cause one to fail? I still can't think of a single example. On the flip side, can misery breed failure? Well, you have a fine example sitting right in front of you. I'm so pathetically miserable, I can't even think straight."

"Well, Sam, you're just starting to make sense. Don't stop!" Charlie joked. So Sam kept talking.

"I don't know why I didn't see this earlier, but now I understand the duality of your argument. I was convinced you were a populist, out for the common man and against management, but you really just want great teamwork, success, and happiness along the way. In life, we're always choosing sides, instead of working together. This failing business here is *our fault*. It's not management's fault, or labor's, or Democrats', or Republicans', or...whatever, take your pick. We're so busy getting at each other's throats, we forget to work together.

"And because we're always in opposition, happiness is kept at bay."

"Bingo!" Charlie exclaimed as he approached Sam, placing a steady, forgiving hand on his shoulder. "There's hope for you yet, my friend. Happiness doesn't follow money, Sam. It's the other way around. Clear out the loud voices and the baggage and the cobwebs from your head, and you'll be able to make money follow happiness. And Sam, you *will* find the solution to Vunorri's problems."

CHAPTER 13

A BROKEN MAN

Sam parked his car and meekly shut the door. He hadn't slept well the night before and was still reeling from his Charlie-induced meltdown. He stared at the Vunorri tower in front of him, frozen. He didn't want to go inside. He dreaded the very idea, his stomach churning, faculties twisted. Never before had he felt this way about a job. Just one foot in front of the other, he thought to himself. "What's wrong with me?" he muttered. A mere three weeks of consulting had turned him into a catatonic puddle of goo. Fighting back tears. He could barely comprehend the implications. His body was not lying to him; it was rejecting Vunorri Inc.

His personal state had been shaken.

As others walked in past him, he feared the worst—that he didn't have the answers Dick needed. Failure was never an option for him, but now it seemed inevitable. This job was not coming together. Would Dick even pay him?

As he walked through the front door, he was greeted by the receptionist. No, wait, he wasn't greeted at all. There she sat...sleeping! It was 8:05 a.m., and her head was cocked back and to the side, with a wee bit of drool escaping the side of her mouth. She was fast asleep as everyone milled by her.

"Unreal," he joked to himself. "How could you not have seen that coming, Sam?" Was anyone going to wake her up? Laughing was all he could do to keep from crying.

Sam left her slovenly presence and headed toward his office. Until he stopped. Something silly had been gnawing at him. Truth be told, he had been lugging around way too many heavy carry-on bags, a plethora of matters on his mind. But for whatever reason, one of the lighter items surfaced.

He had spent hours upon hours out in the factory, and in the warehouse. He had spent more hours than he cared to count in his assigned office, in the lunchroom, on the first floor, up on two, and in the fourth floor Taj Mahal Tower suites insulated from everything that was truly Vunorri Inc. He had never been on the third floor. Why was that? The logical answer was there was nothing there. But what *was* there? Something, surely, and he wanted to know. Sam didn't know why he wanted to know. On top of that, he didn't feel the need to know why he wanted to know. He got on the elevator and pressed "3."

Upon disembarking, the mental picture he had constructed of what the space would look like proved to be way off. Not even close. The entire floor was ghostly. Creepy. Barren. Nothing had been cleaned. Office equipment, chairs, cubes, papers—all abandoned. It was like a time capsule, but one that had been opened and its contents strewn about. Almost like nuclear fallout, with humans replacing the descending radioactive dust. This was where people used to work, until times got tough and three rounds had been executed.

In the whisper quiet of this cubicle landscape, Sam heard a rustling. A noise. What was making noise *up here*? Sam tiptoed, floating across the cheap, industrial carpet until he came upon...

"*Whoa*!" Sam bellowed. "Who are you???"

"David. My name's David."

The young man looked to be in his early 20s. He had hair that curled everywhere and was wearing a blue dress shirt, khakis, and some shiny dress shoes. He looked like a kid working his first office job ever, one who had received some "how to dress up" advice from his parents. Sam found him sitting on the floor, his back against a cubicle, grasping a book.

"Sorry, you scared me," David said.

"You scared *me*! What are you doing up here?"

"They brought me in from the temp service three days ago. But they have nothing for me to do."

"What do you mean? That doesn't make any sense. They brought you here for a reason."

"They said they needed some filing and recordkeeping help. But the CFO doesn't have anything for me. I checked with Human Resources. Everyone keeps saying they're going to have something for me to do soon."

"I don't understand why you're up here," Sam said.

"I was bored out of my mind, so I found this quiet area, and I've been reading. *Anything* to pass the time."

"You're just sitting up here reading a book?"

"They told me to sit tight, they'd have something for me to do soon. I felt weird sitting around, near them, doing nothing. It was making my skin crawl.

"Listen, don't tell them I was up here, OK? It's not my fault. I asked them and asked them and asked them for something to do."

"It's not my job to tell them about you," Sam said. "My job is to turn this place around."

"Does it need turning around?"

"Yeah. It kinda seems like it's headed off a cliff. Finding you up here isn't exactly changing my mind, either."

"How'd you sleep last night?" Charlie asked.

Sam wearily looked at his antagonist. "Like a baby," he answered. "Meaning I was up every two hours, fussy and sad, couldn't get back to sleep. As you might suspect, I had some stuff on my mind."

Sam grabbed a sandwich from the vending machine and sat down.

"Charlie, I wanted to ask you. What exactly was that yesterday—that little act of yours where you egged me on, got me all upset, needling me, pushing my buttons? What was that all about?"

Charlie considered Sam's question for a moment and decided to answer it honestly. He thought Sam deserved that. "I suppose it's like what they claim to do in the military. I had to break you down before I could build you back up. We've been having lunch together for weeks, and I know you want to help Vunorri, and I want you to help Vunorri, but you just weren't getting it. However, you're kinda like Darth Vader. I sensed the good in you." Charlie chuckled a bit at the notion.

"Thanks Luke," Sam joked. "Glad to be your father, I guess."

"Well, I was gonna say you were like a snake and just needed to shed your skin..."

"I'll take the *Star Wars* reference, thanks."

There was a comfort in the air that had certainly not been present the day before—more comfort between them than any previous day. A brief ray of light shone in; for the moment, Sam wasn't a bundle of nerves.

"Sam, I wanted to make a breakthrough with you. I care about this company and want to see it survive."

"But why do you care about this place? Why would you care?"

"I have a lot of time invested here," Charlie said. "It's as much my company as it is anyone else's. You're a very intelligent guy, Sam, with tons of experience. But the people aspect...to me, one piece of you seemed to be missing. There were things I really wanted you to understand—about Vunorri, and about life. Human beings can always do better. We can always be improving. We can always be learning—learning skills, better human relations, life balance, all of that. I wanted you to take this in: humans can be nicer to each other. *That's* the kind of change we should strive for."

"Well, you got my attention," Sam admitted.

"I'm glad. I wanted you to *feel* it. That's how we learn best. I wish we could just study textbooks and 'get it.' I could lecture you all day, and I certainly have. I could've handed you a PowerPoint deck, but what good would that have done? We have to be thrust into life situations in order to really catch the true drift of them. It's unfortunate that we have to be physically placed in the shoes of others before we feel what they feel—before we can empathize with their lot in life. But that's just how we are. We have to see pain—and feel agony—before we can relate. I wish that would change. The world would be a much better place if we'd voluntarily take that walk in the shoes of others."

Sam had to ask. "Charlie, where did you come up with all of this?"

Charlie grinned, paused for a moment, and then dumbfounded Sam with his answer.

"*Star Trek.*"

"I'm serious, Charlie."

"I am, too. Ever watch it?" Sam shook his head no. "Well, you're missing out. Good science fiction gets you thinking about what it means to be human. *Star Trek* changed the way I see the world."

"Even if I didn't have the time, and I don't, I would *make* the time to hear you explain this," Sam said.

Charlie obliged. "There are a lot of real-life lessons buried in the show's stories. On the original series, back in the 60s, Nichelle Nichols played the African-American communications officer Uhura. It was one of the first times a black woman had been depicted on TV as something other than a housekeeper. She was an officer on the bridge of a starship. Isn't that amazing to consider? Then, she and William Shatner really threw everyone a curve ball by having the first interracial kiss on TV."

"I'll bet that shook some people up," Sam said.

"Change is difficult for people, and this was change many didn't agree with. Nichols started receiving horribly hateful fan mail, but studio execs didn't deliver it to her out of fear she'd panic and quit. When she found out they were holding her mail, she submitted her resignation. However, right before his assassination, Martin Luther King Jr.—can you believe it?—convinced her that her role was too important to abandon. She decided to stay. I've always thought about the turmoil of that era, of how much struggle our nation had to go through to make change. And I know this will sound stupid, but there are people just like her here at Vunorri, swimming upstream against a raging current of office politics, racism, mean managers, apathetic coworkers and more. People being mistreated for whatever worthless reasons we come up with."

Sam listened and absorbed. "That doesn't sound stupid to me at all," he said. So Charlie continued.

"Gene Roddenberry, the show's creator, had a vision for a twenty-third and twenty-fourth century world where humanity is all grown up, having evolved into a species with a propensity to get along and care about things other than material possessions and power. Social and personal development was stressed instead. Right now, Sam, I see our workplace here as up for grabs. We're either going to find a way to get along better and prosper, and care about the things we should be caring about—each other—or we're going to go in the other direction. Nothing ever stays the same."

"You want Vunorri to change *like that*?" Sam asked. "I'm not saying it couldn't happen, but..."

"Sam, be skeptical anytime someone rallies against change. Stand up and challenge that. Humanity has a rich history of believing atrocious things, or acting in terrible ways, until all of a sudden, due to protest or necessity or the mere passing of time or just growing up, we suddenly believe something else. You know we used to have witch hunts and burn the ones we caught. We used to prevent women from voting. We used to tell consumers smoking was cool. We used to make black people drink out of a different drinking fountain and give up their bus seats to white people. What in the world was wrong with us? Does any of that sound OK to you, Sam?"

"No, of course not. That's all crazy."

"But all such practices were once common, and that's because the majority in power believed they were *just and correct*. When a minority demanded the abolition of these barbarisms, people kicked and screamed, predicting the downfall of society. Does that sound familiar?"

Sam didn't have to think about it long. "I've been arguing for profit before humans, and you've been surreptitiously trying to convince me it should be the other way around. Then I kicked and screamed and yelled at you like a crazy person." Sam laughed a bit; Charlie broke out in a grin.

"Precisely," Charlie confirmed. "A silly science fiction show reinforced my belief that we humans *can* improve our lot in life. We can change. It may take time. It may take too much time. We'll have our loud detractors. We just have to keep plugging away—showing up, declaring what we believe, and repeating those steps over and over and over again.

"So my question for you, Sam, is, 'Can Vunorri change?' What do you think?"

Sam considered the question carefully. His answer was appropriately a hedge. "I suppose a revolution is possible here, but I'm not sure the bank will care to wait. The numbers just aren't there. Unless I can pull off a miracle, we're toast."

Sam really needed to get back to the interviews and the financials, but he couldn't help but tap his new friend's knowledge and wisdom.

"Charlie, if we were going to go about making this a happier place, how do you think we'd pull it off?"

Charlie wasn't sure how many lunches they had left together, so it was time to lay out his happiness manifesto. "You really want to know what I'd do?" Charlie asked.

Sam nodded.

"Have patience as I walk you through this, OK?" Charlie said. Sam agreed, and Charlie began.

"Are people unhappy at Vunorri because of money? Some might think they should be paid more, or they might be ticked off they haven't received raises. But our problems run so much deeper.

"During these past few weeks, we've deliberated on, and you've discovered, all of the elements necessary to put a turnaround plan into place. Remember when we talked about the lunacy of the workplace?"

"Yeah, you argued that we go to work because we need to support our families and ourselves," Sam said.

"And that we also have the expectation that money will buy us happiness. What else?" Charlie asked.

"You said that, when we can't work well together, we're not happy and can't excel at our jobs."

"Yes, can't excel, and don't want to. You found out firsthand what it's like to possess talent but be unable to get your job done. Your descension into madness, so to speak...how did it come to pass?"

"Terrible things kept happening to me," Sam said. "It seemed like everyone here was out to get me."

"Exactly. You felt that way because Vunorri is brimming with politics, fighting, and silly bickering. Workplaces in general are filled with people different than us. Black and white, Democrat and Republican, rich and poor, management and worker..."

"Consultant and Vunorri employee about to be laid off," Sam interrupted.

"Yes," Charlie acknowledged. "These actual or perceived differences mattered to our employees. And to you. *That* is some rough footing to build a successful company on.

"Then, we have bosses with big heads and lazy agendas and turf to protect. They don't give us employees enough responsibility, don't listen to our ideas, and treat us as expendable parts.

"And then, people find themselves not only failing to work in harmony, but competing with each other. There's no time to work for the common good when I want the promotion instead of you. Office politics—deadly.

"And if all of that wasn't enough, we sometimes have to work with jerks. Some people just aren't nice. Maybe it's how they were brought up. Maybe they just hate life. I don't know. But this gets old real fast. With all of this backstabbing and whatnot, trust and teamwork cannot emerge.

"The result? Are you ready for this?" Charlie asked.

"None of our six human needs are being met," Sam said. "The result is unhappiness."

"Well done, my friend. Unhappy employees are the result. I don't know why we just throw our hands up in the air and say, 'No one's happy at work because, you know, it's work. It's just a job. *Who's happy at work?*' Well, we can be! Why do we tiptoe around discussions about finding happiness at work? Are we afraid if we don't work our people's fingers to the bone, we won't make enough money? Are we afraid the boss will think we're 'soft' because we're talking about our feelings?"

"Probably both," Sam said. "But I think that train's left the station."

"Well, I'm not sure it's left the station, but the conductor is firing up the engines. So, we're meeting with a lack of fulfillment at work, and we're unhappy. The result is two-fold. One, the work we do is substandard. It's difficult to excel when you're unhappy. I believe we capably proved that yesterday," Charlie said with a sly grin. "This is a *big* problem for the companies we work for. Substandard work means we're not generating as much profit as we could be."

Sam's little light bulb finally glowed. "Discordant workplaces yield unhappiness. Unhappiness yields poor work performance, which yields lower productivity and lower profits. Which yields even more unhappiness. Wash, rinse, repeat. Awful. There's your ROI of happiness at work!"

"You got it," Charlie said. "The second thing, and this is the worst. You're a despondent person at work, and every day, you jump in the car at five o'clock and go home to see your family. That should cheer you up, right? But you're in a terrible mood! Many of us take our work unhappiness home and barf it out onto our families. So home life gets worse. Then you go back to work with more venom, for more venom. It's a terrible cycle to get caught up in, right?"

Sam nodded in approval. "My home life has suffered these past few weeks," he said.

Charlie continued. "What a true horror that is, maybe the real tragedy of all of this. Where's the next generation of amazing human beings going to come from? They should be emerging from the households of happy parents. But instead, they're scraping by in the households of stressed-out workers who come home breathing fire after a long day at the office. Today's job stress creates tomorrow's greatest generation? I don't think so. And those kids subsequently come to think of work as a necessary evil. The cycle continues.

"So, we have underperforming companies and underperforming families. Sam, this is why I care so much about happiness in the workplace."

"I'm with you," Sam said.

"So let me ask you—how can we send parents home in a better mood? And how can we construct a workplace foundation to stand on that'll allow us to excel?"

Sam took a confident stab at it. "We need to care about happiness at work."

"Yes, Sam! Caring about happiness, not as some afterthought or empty hope. Caring about happiness *first*—that's what we need. It's what we all deserve. The workplace is a symphony of complacency, backstabbing, laziness, and selfishness. And Vunorri is Beethoven's 6th—the perfect symphony. No wonder most people here hate their jobs."

"Most people I meet," Sam said, "aren't happy at work."

Charlie nodded in agreement. "There's always money to be made, Sam. There's always a tactic to be plied. There's always a new product to be introduced. There's always a new location to be opened. But what *don't* we always have? Happiness. Again, care about happiness *first*. Then you can move on to your tactics; they'll all be there waiting for you."

Charlie then reached the apogee of his explanation. "Most of our problems would be solved, or at least would never resurface, if we created a culture here at Vunorri in which our employees focused on being good to each other. Happiness would be the result.

"We've talked about a lot here, but let's bring it home. To make the change we want to see—happy people working good jobs with kind coworkers, a Vunorri where job happiness is possible—we're going to have to shock the system. We have to shoehorn it in, one way or another. And I don't care what any management guru thinks about this. Kindness and happiness need to be added to the bottom line of this workplace, starting now.

"Somehow, Sam, you have to *make* that happen. We need some 'rules of the road.' Codify kindness and create happiness here, ASAP.

Charlie finally stopped. "Sorry, I talked for too long. I'm done."

Sam sat there, kind of stunned. Stunned at his epiphany. Charlie made it all make sense. All of the lectures, all of the blathering about happiness and kindness. It was now all clear to him. Codify kindness. How interesting. No, the bank probably wasn't going to accept Charlie's treatise on how unhappiness is born and what it does to people and businesses, and Dick would never buy it, but Sam was glad anyway to have heard it. He could not have been more impressed. Humbled by the man in the mailroom.

"Vunorri's ship might still be sunk," Sam said, "but at least now I understand your point of view. I get where you're coming from and it's hard to disagree."

Sam immediately began churning through his newly acquired database of beliefs, thinking of how to translate some of it into a turn-around plan for Vunorri. However, one little thing didn't compute. Charlie's work duties and his apparent intellect were incongruous.

"Charlie, why are you doing this job?" Sam asked.

"What do you mean by that?" Charlie responded.

"Well, you once challenged me about my purpose. Now it's my turn. You have wisdom to spare. You're in the *mailroom*. I don't understand."

Looking puzzled, but understanding exactly where Sam was headed, Charlie asked, "What should you have me do instead?"

"Charlie, you could *lead* this place. You could lead a company! You could be in management."

"And why would you have me work such a position?"

"I mean...the pay."

"And do you feel as though I need more money?"

"Well, I..."

Charlie seemed to be enjoying this. "And what exactly is the point of me changing jobs? What's the point of what I do? Do you think that my life requires more money or greater status in order for me to feel fulfillment and achieve happiness? What am I missing here?"

"Well, you could be doing more with your talents. By your definition, wouldn't that be, like, a contribution to humanity?" Sam asked in a somewhat mocking tone.

"Well, Sam, we've had many discussions over the last three weeks, and I feel like I've kinda helped *you*. Maybe that's my way of helping.

"My six human needs are more or less met here—and outside of work, too. I'm a happy guy. Go fulfill your human needs, Sam, and convince everyone here at Vunorri to do it, too.

"Here's a great place to start. One of my favorite quotes is from Maya Angelou. Do you know who that is?"

"I've heard of her," Sam responded.

"She was a famous civil right activist. There's one of her quotes that I'll always know by heart. It's a great building block with which to build a life. 'People will forget what you said. People will forget what you did. But people will never forget how you made them feel.' How does that make *you* feel to hear that?"

Sam thought about it for a minute. "I think what you mean is that there's more to life than what we do. We can achieve this or that, but we should never forget that everything we do makes people *feel* a certain way. So make those people feel great—that's the foundation for a good life."

"*Yes!*" Charlie exclaimed. "And *nothing* is more critical than living your life on a solid foundation. People are so unhappy here at Vunorri. It's terrible and so unnecessary. We make a great product. We really do. But everyone here acts in ways that make their fellow employee feel dead inside. So that needs to change now. Enough with merely surviving. We have to thrive. Fulfill those six human needs, or else prepare for trouble."

"Oh, I think I've found trouble," Sam said.

"I'll let you go, Sam—I know you need to get back to it. I'll leave you with this question: Here at Vunorri, have we built a workplace we can be proud of?"

Without hesitation, Sam said, "No, you have not."

"Then we have all of our work still ahead of us."

Sam looked down and frowned at his gelatinous meal. "By the way, *what is this* I'm eating out of the vending machine? It tastes like gruel! You'd think we were in prison!"

Charlie caught the irony. "A rather poignant thing to say..."

CHAPTER 14

ARMAGEDDON

With seven days remaining in the engagement, Sam had so much and yet so little. After all those lunches, the countless annoying conversations, the sizable meltdown, and the resulting soul searching, Charlie had pulled off a personality coup of preposterous proportions. Sam viewed his work, his life, and his role in the lives of others in a whole new way. He felt better about himself and more optimistic about the world around him. He'd be able to give all sorts of excellent new advice during future engagements.

But what of Vunorri? He had reams of notes—a laundry list of go-do's that he could give Dick. *Everything* needed fixing! But did he really have any answers? The bank sure wanted answers. They wanted their money, and would start foreclosure proceedings on the business in a little over a week. If this was a midnight deadline, the clock read 11:45 p.m. Tick, tick, tick. Sam was always able to help a company when he wasn't under pressure and could control the conditions around him. But this was a panic-button, call-in-the-cavalry situation, and Vunorri was running out of time.

He had his own assigned office and his own gigantic desk, covered entirely with decks and financial reports and paper and *nothing*. All of this information might as well have been tossed in a wood chipper. *Where was the answer?* Sam's head was heavy, and spinning; he was exhausted, and having trouble focusing on anything except feeling miserable. Time for a walk to try to clear his head.

The factory was buzzing with activity. It all made for a sort of white noise that was more comforting to Sam than the low buzz of the fluorescent bulbs in his office. Sam liked walking through the factory. Out here, he found peace in the process, the making of things, the hustle and bustle of entrepreneurship. Melinda and her cruel fiefdom, Neil and his dirty face and horrible attitude...none of that mattered out here. Without these factory artisans, building what they build, everything dies.

"Sam, hey! How are you?" asked several line workers.

"Good, guys, How goes it?"

"Another day, another dollar. How's your work going?"

Sam wanted to tell them the truth. He wanted to confide in someone. To him, it seemed like he was holding down the lid on the about-to-explode powder keg. But he didn't want to alarm these guys. At this hour, none of this really seemed to be their fault.

"The project's OK. I'm finding a lot." Sam's face did not lie, though.

"We heard you yelling in the lunchroom. It's not going so good, is it?" they asked. These guys were no dummies. Sam tried to make small talk and change the subject, picking up a part off the assembly line.

"What's this 'Sciencetronik' company? I see crates from them up to the ceiling over in the warehouse."

"They're our largest supplier. They're a total pain in the butt. We're often out of their materials. They hold our shipments hostage until we pay them."

Sam froze. "Wait, what? I hadn't heard anything about that. Who orders this stuff?"

"The accounting guy. Man, he's crazy. I don't ask him no questions."

Sam was confused. Why was Neil ordering raw materials? That was not, or at least should not have been his job. And why hadn't Sam found this out until now? He quickly made his way back to his office.

He grabbed Vunorri's financials and stared at one number: *"Cost of goods sold."* He had reviewed the job costing models, the factory processes, the org chart, and the Profit and Loss statement. But what was in that Cost of Goods number? He was a retired auditor. *Why hadn't he tested that number?* Why hadn't he scrutinized it? He ran to Accounting.

"Josie, can you print for me the general ledger activity for Cost of Goods Sold for the last three months?"

"I can't, I'm not supposed to. Neil controls that."

"Oh come on!" Sam said as he threw his arms up in the air, walking away in disgust. How was he supposed to get anything done with *Neil's* help? Sam wanted nothing to do with him and vice versa.

Then, his days as a CPA and engagements past came rushing back to him. Why would Josie, a controller, not be allowed to print reports out of the general ledger? That made no sense. By the time Sam got back to his office, he was feeling uneasy, and then panicky. Something wasn't right.

To do his digging, Sam needed some accounts payable reports. Since there was apparently no way he was going to get any help from Accounting on this, Sam sprinted to the IT department. Out of breath upon arrival, he found the IT manager in the server room.

"Hey, Jeremy, remember me?" Sam asked, speaking very quickly. "I interviewed you last week? I need some accounts payable information."

"Why aren't you over in Accounting for this?" Jeremy deadpanned.

"Long story, listen, can you run a report for me with Vunorri's top ten vendors by purchase volume and a list of our purchases from them for the past year?"

"Our computer system won't do that," Jeremy responded.

"Jeremy, I *need* the information. Can you write a script to pull the information into a report? It doesn't need to be pretty. I just need the data—names, invoice numbers, PO numbers, dates, and dollar amounts."

"Yes, but I'm not supposed..."

"How long will it take you?" Sam blurted out.

"I can...I don't know, maybe an hour?"

"*Do it!* I need it in 15 minutes. Shut your door and get it done. I'll be back."

Jeremy looked unsure of what typhoon just blew into IT, or why he was taking orders from a consultant, but the look in Sam's eye said, "Get this done immediately."

Sam took the report back to the conference room and looked it over. Not surprisingly, it was full of Sciencetronik invoices. Sam quickly picked ten large paid invoices and asked Josie to pull them.

"Here they are, Sam. But I couldn't find two of 'em."

"Please go look for them again," Sam said. "And please bring me your purchase order log."

The missing invoices had already been paid, so Josie should have been able to find them.

"I looked everywhere, but...I don't know, maybe they got misfiled. We paid one of these recently. It could be in Neil's office. Do you want me to go ask him?"

"*No*. No need. Is that the purchase order log?"

In the log, Sam found the PO number for the newer invoice referenced on the general ledger report. It wasn't a Sciencetronik purchase order.

"Josie, the PO number for this invoice doesn't even correspond to your PO log. What's going on here?"

"That's weird. I don't..."

"I need you to pull the cancelled check on these two for me," Sam said.

"I'll go look for the older one. For the newer one, we don't have that bank statement yet. Should be coming in the mail in the next day or two."

Sam stared at the general ledger report and wasn't feeling too good about what he was seeing. Two missing invoices? And wrong PO numbers? To make sure he wasn't going crazy, he called Sciencetronik.

"Hi, this is Sam Maslow with Vunorri. I'm calling with some questions on two invoices. Can you assist me?"

"Sir, I don't have your name in our system as an authorized representative of Vunorri. I'm sorry, but I can't give you any information."

"Hold on..." Sam called Josie in. "Josie, I'm on the line with Sciencetronik. Tell this lady to talk to me." Josie obliged.

The Sciencetronik rep was now ready to cooperate. "OK sir, what can I help you with?"

"Here's the first one. Invoice 134687 for $36,200.23. I can't find our paper copy anywhere. Can you e-mail me a copy of this invoice?"

"Hold on, sir." After about a minute, she came back on the line. "Sir, this invoice number is not one of your invoices. Can you read the number back to me again?"

Sam again read her the invoice number, amount, date, and purchase order number. "That's *not* a Vunorri invoice, sir. I'm not allowed to tell you which of our customers it was for, but it wasn't Vunorri. I'm sorry, sir."

"That can't be right," Sam said. "I'm looking at it right here. We paid it three weeks ago with check 2506. Can you check the invoice numbers around it? Maybe our payables person transposed a number."

"I don't see one of your invoices even near that invoice number you provided me. In fact, I'm searching here, and I don't even see that dollar amount in our system. Not for you, not for any vendor." The other invoice was also a mystery—not in Sciencetronik's system.

"OK thanks, bye," and he hung up the phone. Josie returned.

"Sam, that older missing invoice...I can't find the canceled check. I searched the entire bank statement for that month. It's not in there. I don't understand."

Sam's mind raced. This was definitely not good. He didn't even want to consider what he had just found—or didn't find. He didn't want to believe his gut. But he had to go down this rabbit hole. He needed to find check 2506.

The mail! Josie said the bank statement might be coming in the next day or two. Sam ran to the mailroom.

"Charlie, has today's mail come yet?"

"Yeah, Sam, it's all right here. I haven't sorted it yet."

Sam looked for a big thick envelope—the bank statement and all of last month's cancelled checks. There it was!

"But Sam I can't let you..."

"Save it," Sam shot back as he made a 'talk to the hand' gesture while departing the mailroom.

Sam ran back to his office and ripped open the envelope. The bank did not sort the checks by number, so he had to look through all of them. Hundreds of checks, mostly computer-run checks. He was looking for a manual check. It looked different than the computer checks. He start rifling through the stack, one by one, but it was taking too long. His heart pounding, he set the pile down and fanned them out across the big table.

Found it!

Check 2506, a handwritten check for $36,200.23.

Made out to Neil. The check was paid to the order of Neil.

"Oh my god! This cannot be happening," he shouted aloud as he pounded the table with his fist, attracting the attention of practically everyone in the nearby accounting department. The missing check was made out to Neil. For maybe five seconds, his brain tried to explain away the truth, but what other explanation was there? With a single check, Neil had stolen over thirty-six thousand dollars from Vunorri.

Sam felt ill, cold—it was suddenly freezing in his office. He was shell-shocked, absolutely no idea what to do next. Confront Neil? Call the police? Go get Dick? Sam's ruckus had caused a small group to gather outside the room. Sam felt their eyes on him as they peered in, and he tried to pull himself together.

He grabbed the general ledger report and the check and ran up the stairs to The Tower. He was sweating profusely as he knocked on Dick's door.

"Sam, good to see you. What's the matter? You're out of breath."

"Dick, you're not going to believe this." He showed him the check.

"I don't understand," Dick said. "What am I looking at here?

"Dick, this 36,000 dollar check is made out to Neil!" Sam held the check up to Dick's face. "This is a fake Sciencetronik invoice that he paid to himself!"

"Paid to himself? I don't understand. That's impossible!" Dick exclaimed. "Sam, what is going on?"

"Dick, Neil is *stealing* from you. He's embezzling from Vunorri!!!"

"Oh dear lord...How?"

It was a handwritten check, signed by Dick, made out to Neil. Neil had been putting a clear piece of tape over the 'Pay to the order of' section, and writing Sciencetronik's name there. Dick never noticed the tape. After Dick signed it, Neil gingerly pulled the tape up, and made out the check to himself. Then he pulled the incriminating cancelled check out of the monthly bank statement when it arrived, eliminating the evidence.

Sam was beside himself. "Dick, how often do *you* talk to this vendor?"

"Never, really. Neil insists on handling the weekly negotiations with them. We owe Sciencetronik a lot of money. They demand a check once a week in order to release our weekly shipment. Sometimes more than one check a week. We have to FedEx them the check or they don't ship to us. No shipment and we're shut down. He keeps their shipments coming to us."

"I don't believe it!" Sam exclaimed. "I don't believe it! Call the police. Call the police right now, Dick!"

Sam ran out of the office and down the stairwell, back to the accounting department. Neil was not there. All of his employees knew something was up. And then Sam's eyes betrayed him, because he coulda swore he saw Neil, outside in the parking lot. He squinted his eyes to focus, as if that would help, and did a double take. Everyone saw it—Neil in a laughable sprint toward his car. "Oh my God," Sam said aloud. "He's running. *He's running!*"

Josie approached. "What's going on, Sam?"

Dick then arrived in Accounting. "I called them. They're sending a squad car."

"He just left the building," Sam said. "I saw him leave. He ran..."

"Where was he going?" Dick asked.

"Dick, where do you think he was going??? He knew I was on to him. He's been intercepting the mail, grabbing the monthly bank statement, and pulling the forged checks out. He must've freaked when I grabbed the mail today and started tearing through last month's cancelled checks."

"This is just impossible," Dick said, looking white as a ghost. "How could he do this? How much did he take?"

"I have no idea, Dick! I just caught him ten minutes ago! Get a forensic accountant in here. Oh, son of a...your insurance. Dick, do you have a crime policy?"

"I handle our insurance," Josie said. "Yes, we have a crime policy."

Sam wanted to feel relieved, but this *was* Vunorri Inc., after all. Anything was possible. "Call your agent," Sam said. "Get them over here."

Sam was disgusted—nearly physically ill at this point. His stomach was volcanic. His white dress shirt was drenched, and he smelled like he had spent an afternoon in the humid summer outdoors. If that insurance policy didn't cover this, Vunorri would have to pursue Neil to the end of the earth for that money, and that was only if they could fend off the bank. Unreal—how much money was it? Was Neil killing the margins himself? It did not matter how great a sleuth Sam was—he just wished none of this had ever happened.

It was 4:00 p.m. and he had not even had lunch. Wasn't hungry. Besides catching a sticky-fingered CFO in the act, Sam not eating lunch was almost equally weird.

And then, it was as if the blindfold had come off. He could see all. Focus took hold. This job was done. He was steaming angry. No company had ever been as jacked up as Vunorri. For Sam, now, *this* was the principle of the thing. It wasn't about great business practices, money, not any of that crap he used to worship. Now, the horrible quagmire of Vunorri had him to the brink. It was time to do what he promised Dick he was going to do: tell it to him straight.

Sam found Dick in his office, slumped in his wingback chair.

"Dick, clear your schedule tomorrow morning. It's report day. I'll meet you here at eight o'clock."

"But Sam, there's still another week to go."

"I've seen enough. 8:00 a.m. Be here. Don't be late," and he stormed off. He was disgusted by Dick's countenance, Dick's office, Dick's cluelessness, everything. He left quickly so he wouldn't say something he'd later regret.

Sam went home to prepare his report. He stayed up till 4:30 a.m., writing and compiling. He was a demon. Never had the work flowed like this. He was possessed.

Fifty pages later, he was ready to lower the boom. He couldn't wait to exhale this indictment onto Dick's face.

CHAPTER 15

INDICTMENT

D-DAY HAD ARRIVED. TWO HOURS OF SLEEP, A COLD SHOWER, A Quad Mocha, a scathing 50-page report and a whole fistful of anger—that's what Sam had to work with on this dark, cloudy Friday morning. He rarely got stage fright when presenting to a client, but these were obviously different circumstances. He wasn't operating at 100% capacity, and he knew it. Nervous, shell-shocked, weary, and furious. Would he be able to collect his thoughts and convince Dick things needed to change? At this point, did it even matter if Dick "got it?"

"Good morning Sam, come on in," Dick said in a warm tone. "How are you this morning? Can I get you anything?"

"No, I'm fine. Let's get this show on the road."

"Sam, are you sure? You look a little punchy."

"I'll survive. Where are we gonna do this?"

They proceeded to an open conference room in The Tower, Dick guiding Sam with a hand on his shoulder. Sam was suddenly a "you're violating my personal zone" kind of guy. Punchy was an understatement.

"Sam, before we get started, I wanted to thank you for what you did yesterday...catching Neil."

"It's fine," Sam said dismissively.

"No, Sam, you deserve credit. We don't even know how much he stole, but I have forensic accountants showing up later today. Your discovery saved my company. Hot diggity, the bank's gonna *love* this!"

Sam wanted to get this over with, and his nerves were starting to boil more and more as Dick exuberantly talked. "Dick, thanks. Glad to have helped. Now let's get started."

Sam pulled two 50-page reports out of his briefcase and passed one across the table to Dick, whose eyes popped wide open when he felt the heft of the deck. "Sam, what's in this?" Dick jokingly asked.

"Dick, what do you think's in it??? I just caught a criminal in this place yesterday! One who could've been easily stopped if anyone had been paying attention! You think that's your only problem? Open the report!"

Sam proceeded to take Dick apart. Firing all ordnances, lighting him up. He walked Dick through each department, detailing countless incidents, terrible accounting, breakdowns in internal controls, unpaid sales commissions, intimidation tactics, psychological abuse, high turnover, lack of oversight, employees crying, phones as missiles, embezzlement! Basically utter chaos in nearly every corner of the company. Sam kept going and going—he was a bottomless pit of damning evidence.

Dick had clearly been knocked off balance by Sam's energetic, angry presentation. While he was not a control freak, no one likes to be the center of so much negative attention, and most people do not like being yelled at. He remained silent, listening, until Sam paused to catch his breath. "So much of what you're saying...I didn't even know it was going on," Dick said. "Why didn't anybody tell me?"

"Why didn't you go *ask*?" Sam retorted. "Why didn't you hire better? Why didn't you demand more out of these capable people? Why have the good ones left and the mediocre ones stayed? Why are cruel people like Insane Melinda allowed to rule like a despot here? Why wasn't Neil asked to update those job cost reports? Why is 'Don't bring me any surprises' the management credo here? Why didn't you *lead*? Who's driving the bus here, Dick?"

Dick didn't have a word to say. Sam wasn't done.

"And why is this all about money for you?" That struck a nerve.

"Hey, that's not fair," Dick responded.

"Fair??? What's fair anymore, Dick? You've been bonusing yourself and yourself alone, while salaries have been frozen for years."

"What's that got to do with anything?"

"You said it—the first day I was in here! You hadn't bonused yourself last year. *Bonus*??? You laid people off three times over the past five years! You don't get a cookie for that! What kind of message do you think you're sending with this kind of behavior? You can't build teams this way! Your dad did all the hard work, and you won the sperm lottery, huh! Calling me was the first smart thing you've done in years. I mean, do you realize what a *dolt* you've been?"

Dick turned a nice shade of red. "Is that really how you see me?"

"It's not just you; it's this whole company! Dick, I have experience inside hundreds of organizations. This is the *worst* place I've ever been. By far! You might get a reprieve from the bank because of the Neil situation, but Vunorri Inc. is going to die anyway unless some big changes occur."

"But the crime insurance...we'll get our money."

"No, no, *no*, Dick! You think busting Neil is your Get Out Of Jail Free card? You might get the line of credit paid down, and maybe if you get a good CPA in here, those job cost models can finally be updated.

But the same squalid conditions will still exist: no oversight, no one working to reach any goals, no kindness. Vunorri's still gonna be a lousy place to work. Your employees are miserable today, and they're going to remain miserable. Do you know why that's a problem, Dick?

"I had a complete and thorough mental breakdown in your lunchroom the other day! Did you hear about that? I was freaking out. I couldn't think straight. I had no idea what was wrong with the financials, was dreading my own failure, and had *zero* mental capacity to devote to the work of solving the puzzle. Now look, I'm a smart guy, right? Best turnaround consultant in town? My misery had reduced me to a drooling blob. Totally worthless. Me! My brain was scrambled eggs. I was shocked."

"That doesn't sound like you," Dick said.

"Dick, *I wasn't me!* Once I was able to settle myself down, I figured it out. I finally saw the light. We'll spend nearly 100,000 hours of our life working. Do you want to make it a happy 100,000 hours? In an unhappy work environment, most employees, talented or not, will struggle with the exact same problem I did—they won't be able to even think straight, much less do their jobs well. Do you see the point I'm making? If you want your employees to excel on your behalf, you're going to have to create a different kind of workplace where people can be happy.

"There are people inside these walls battling. Battling for a better work life, fighting against the grain—the institutional molasses, lousy management, sometimes utter cruelty, and fellow employees who don't care. They're yearning to do a good job. It's a tough life for the good people. The good ones lose faith and just go limp—what is there to gain for them?

"But Dick, here's the worst part. If the culture of this company doesn't take a turn for the better, you can try to go to sleep at night knowing that Vunorri Inc. is helping to *ruin families*. People take their Vunorri misery home, Dick! This place kills them by day, and they can't pull it together on their short commute home. It's impossible! They take that misery home to their families. That's the true horror of an unhappy work life. And..."

"Now hold on, stop it right there," Dick said. He looked down at the table in front of him, constructing what he wanted to say. It took him 20 long seconds. "You just said something there, my friend...you hit the nail on the head. For me, anyway." He paused again; it was getting more difficult for him to say what he wanted to say as his emotions bubbled to the surface.

Then, he let it all go. "You probably can't tell, but I'm a wreck, Sam," his voice cracking. "Miserable just like you. Except, it seems your misery started about three weeks ago when you arrived here. I've been unhappy for years. Just like you, I don't want to be here. It's a wretched, pitiful grind of a place. Only problem is I have nowhere else to go. There's no escape. Our entire life—all of our money—is wrapped up in this business. I take insecurity, anger, and shame that we're not making more money home to my wife and kids every single day. So not only do I not look forward to coming to work, I don't really look forward to going home, either.

"I'm just so down. And I can't shake it. No amount of money helps. I thought it would, but I'm still depressed. It frightens me.

"And I'm just not my dad. I'm not good with people; I'm not comfortable managing people like he was. I don't have the magic touch like him. He's too kind a man to say anything to me, but I know he knows it. And it kills me inside. I don't measure up."

Sam tried to comfort Dick with words he actually meant. "Maybe you don't measure up...in certain ways. But in other ways, you excel.

Stop beating yourself up about this stuff and just be you. And treat people like you'd want to be treated. It's not that tough."

Dick sighed. "I've let my dad down. I can't imagine a pain worse than this."

"Dick, what do you think is going to make you happy in life? What's going to fill up your cup? Have you ever thought about this? Is it 'stuff?' Material possessions? Power? Legacy? *Why* do you do what you do? *That's* the question you don't have a good answer to right now. I can tell you this: your consumption-based happiness is a false floor you're standing on. And they're false stairs you're climbing. So much reaping, Dick. Where is the sowing?

"You can pursue profits and maximize profits, and squeeze this place dry and take as much out of here as you possibly can. But then what? What happens after that? What is your purpose?

"Dick, you got some great people here at Vunorri, and you can be great, too. You can make as much money as you want to make, but don't you want your employees to be happy doing it? Don't *you* want to be happy?"

Dick was overcome with emotion—disgusted. Sam's words were a smack in the face. He didn't want to believe everything he was hearing, just like Sam hadn't wanted to believe, but he could not refute any of Sam's assertions. And then, he turned to thoughts of his mother, and what she would have thought of all of this. A tear rolled down his cheek; those reflections were too heavy for him to bear.

"I have heard *enough*!" Dick emphatically said, slamming the table. For a brief moment, Sam thought his goose might be cooked. Had he gone overboard during his presentation?

"Big changes need to happen *ASAP*!" Dick said. "I refuse to live like this anymore. We need a better working environment, starting now! No one is going to be happy here at Vunorri until we set some ground rules for how we treat each other!"

Sam leaked a mini-grin. He had just made Dick shed his skin. He had learned from the master. And now it was time to present his big idea.

"I think I can help," Sam said.

"I'm all ears. What do you have in mind?" Dick asked.

"Turn to page 45—I think you're going to like what you see. You said it already. We can take steps to make this a better place to work, but first you guys have to commit to do it. How can you commit to each other? I have an idea. I've never tried anything like this before, but the problems here are so acute and all-encompassing, and time is not on our side. I think we need an unorthodox solution. We need a code to live by. A work code of conduct. Sort of like 'The Vunorri Way.' We have to *make* the change we want to see happen, but we don't have time to let it happen naturally. We have to jumpstart the process."

"That sounds interesting," Dick said. "But how can we pull it off? Where do we even begin?"

"Dick, like I said, this has been a berserk three weeks here. And it's all in my notebook. I kept very detailed notes of everything I witnessed, learned, and felt. Let's go incident by incident, interview by interview, and create little credos—almost like rules, but more like suggestions—guidelines on how to treat each other. Let's use this code to encourage Vunorri employees to respect the work process, to respect each other, and to establish happiness as a main goal. Happiness is elusive at Vunorri due to some big problems, no doubt, but there's a lot of little stuff going on, too. We have to not only encourage people to do good around here, but we also need to *avoid* doing some things that tend to upset people and cause unhappiness. We have to build a workplace we can be proud of."

"Sam, I think it's a great idea. What do we have to lose? Think about it: *what do we have to gain?*"

Sam finally felt at ease saying this. "Dick, you have your happiness to gain."

CHAPTER 16

DRAWING A LINE IN THE SAND

NEEDLESS TO SAY, THURSDAY AND FRIDAY HAD BEEN TWO roller coaster days at Vunorri Inc. The Neil caper, followed by Sam's manifesto, and culminating in Dick having a change of heart and seeing the light. After Sam and Dick agreed that a work code of conduct might turn things around for the company, they began brainstorming on it straight away. A few hours on Friday night led into an 18-hour Saturday and a 16-hour Sunday. The work sessions were long and arduous, but they bore fruit. It was time for the big reveal.

First thing Monday morning, Dick sent out an all-employee e-mail:

"Company meeting, today 10 a.m., warehouse, MANDATORY. We have big news to share."

Employees talked nervously among themselves. Was management going to give people more details on Neil's theft? Was this an announcement of a fourth round of layoffs? No one had a clue as to what was about to go down, and that had everyone biting their nails.

Sam and Dick finalized their materials and prepped the audio system. As 10 o'clock approached, the warehouse began filling up as employees milled in. Dick was going to lead the meeting, and he was apprehensive. Of course he had spoken in front of the company before, but he was never terribly comfortable doing it. And of course, this was ten times the stage—this one counted. The future of the company was on the line. Sam was nervous, too, and after weeks of stress and the long working weekend, he was running on fumes. Still, he was proud of what Dick was about to present, and thankful to Charlie for his role in opening their eyes. Sam scanned the crowd for Charlie, hoping he'd be there to witness Dick's transformation, but couldn't find him among the masses.

Once everyone was settled, Dick walked to the front of the warehouse, grabbed the microphone, and began.

"Good morning, everyone. Thank you very much for being here. First, let me start off by reassuring you. I am not here to announce a fourth round of layoffs." The expected collective sigh of relief...

"No, we're not out of the financial woods yet, but we have a plan. We've got a lot of exciting things to share with you today, so thanks in advance for your patience and your attention.

"By now, I'm sure you've all heard about what Sam found last Thursday. I'm probably not supposed to say much, but..." Dick paused for a moment to at least try to choose his words carefully. "Sam found a large Vunorri check made out to Neil. So we're fairly certain he's been stealing from us. We don't know how much, but we're working on finding out. And we anticipate that our insurance policy is going to provide us a settlement for the stolen funds. We're hopeful that money will get the bank off our back." Murmurs in the room meant the gathered employees found that bit of information rather interesting.

"The reason I mention the bank is that we're about a week away from a deadline of theirs. I need to give them a plan to turn this company around, or they're going to foreclose on us—take the company." Audible gasps filled the warehouse.

"Guys, what happened?" Dick continued. "Neil should never have stolen from us! Really, he should've never been allowed to steal. My hunch is he embezzled hundreds of thousands of dollars from our company. Many of us have been negligent here at Vunorri, asleep at the wheel, but no one more than me. *No one* is more at fault than me! It makes me sick to my stomach to even think about it.

"Do you know how many raises you didn't get because Neil was stealing from Vunorri? Robbing us blind and I had little care to provide him any oversight." Dick looked up to the high ceiling for a minute, perhaps seeking a sign from some higher power. "How many *good* people did I lay off because I...?"

Dick was visibly shaken by his own words. He wondered if anyone could tell his knees were knocking. Sweat was forming on his brow. But he felt spiritually solid—his thoughts were flowing. He was letting go.

"And not only are we a cash-poor failure of a business, but this company is a miserable place to work! Even I can't stand coming to work in the morning. Every single day is a clock-watching death march to five o'clock for me and no doubt for you too. When you think about it, why are we doing this?

"Did you know that, if you spend a career here at Vunorri, you'll spend almost 100,000 hours within these walls, with each other, working side by side? Why can't that be an enjoyable 100,000 hours? Why do things have to stay the way they are now? We can change.

"Here's the worst part of all. This place has had an awful effect on my family. I know it's done the same to you. I go home such a grump, my wife wants nothing to do with me. My kids, even my son who works here, think that work is a necessary evil. That's how I'm raising them—to assume those 100,000 hours are a waste of time you just have to hack through.

"I want my son to have a great place to work in the future. I want you guys to have a job here—a job you like!" At this point, you really could hear that proverbial pin drop in the warehouse. Everyone was shocked. What had gotten into Dick? No one had ever seen this side of him. They were listening intently.

"I believe in our company, in what my dad started. I love what my dad built. For whatever reason—money, vanity, pride, or just the principle of the thing, I want it to go on. But I'm letting him down!"

Dick's voice cracked hard, and his body sagged as he covered his face with his right hand. He lowered the microphone in the other hand, not knowing what to say next. He wasn't sure he'd ever be able to live down a crying fit in front of the entire company, but he could not help but shed a tear. The warehouse remained whisper quiet.

"I've really let my dad down. I'm glad my mom isn't here to see this. But guys, most of all, I've let *you* down. I know some of you don't want to be here anymore, and that's my fault. I know some of you would leave if you could find a different job, but there's nothing out there. It breaks my heart that I run a company at which even *one of you* feels trapped. I heard enough from your interviews with Sam that…I'm just so ashamed."

Sam observed the faces in the crowd, and he could tell that Dick was connecting. All eyes were on him; no one was playing around on their smartphones…people continued to listen.

"Big changes need to happen *now*," Dick said resolutely. "We can't let things go on the way they've been. And that's why I've called you here today. We need to live by a new credo—respect for the work process, respect for the business, and most of all, respect for each other. All of this points to one singular, new goal—happiness. Yes, we need to be more productive and all that, but Vunorri Inc. must become a happier place to work.

"I didn't have the foggiest idea how we could affect such a big change so quickly, but Sam came up with a wonderful idea that's worth a shot. We've developed something—he and I spent the entire weekend working on it. The idea is a little unconventional, but as Sam showed me, it's kind of 'code blue' time for our company. Dire problems call for bold solutions.

"We've created a new tool, and this isn't merely some flavor of the month or management fad. This isn't one random offsite team-building exercise. It's much more than that. It's a work code of conduct called The Happywork Agreement. It includes commitments that me and my management team are going to make to you. It also includes commitments you're going to make back to us. And then there are commitments we'll make together. Forty-six commitments in all. Sounds like a lot, but it's a quick read."

"Our goal is to eliminate apathy, break down barriers, foster communication, and forget our differences. We need to open wide the lines of communication between worker and management. By not working together in harmony, we're slowing ourselves down. And if the bank's repeated phone calls to me prove anything, it's that we don't have any time to waste. We can do better, guys!

"Think of these commitments as 'words to live by' or 'happiness rules of the road.' We're going to start treating each other better—*now*. This is what life is going to be like at Vunorri going forward. Now's the time to be productive and happy. We've got to eliminate the biases, bottlenecks, sticking points, sniping, and productivity destroyers that permeate this place.

"Do you guys get what I'm saying? We don't have to hurt this much! The pain we're all feeling can be avoided. We just have to reorganize our priorities. Not change our priorities. Just change the order. From now on, happiness comes first. I'm not living another day here in misery. *No more*!" Many employees nodded in agreement.

"Before I say anything else, I want to take a moment to acknowledge Sam. I brought him in here three weeks ago, and in that short time, he's been through a lot. Vunorri isn't an easy place to be, but Sam, you really stuck with it. Thank you for discovering the theft, thank you for your tireless efforts, and thank you for opening my eyes to what's really important in life. You may have saved our company." The gathered masses began clapping, which Sam had not seen coming. He gave Dick a nod of appreciation.

Dick then noticed a hand go up in the middle of the gathered crowd. "Yes sir?" Dick asked.

"Mr. Vunorri, can we *see* The Happywork Agreement?"

"Dick smiled and said, "Of course you can! Sam?" Sam grabbed the pile of handouts and began distributing them.

"Sam is passing around copies of The Happywork Agreement. We want you to take about 15 minutes to read through it, and then we'll gather up after that. Sound OK?

"Good. Thanks again for your time, everyone. Have a good read, and I'll be back in about 15." Dick set the microphone down and joined Sam off to the side. With that, Vunorri's employees began reading through The Happywork Agreement.

VUNORRI INC.

THE HAPPYWORK AGREEMENT

THIS IS A WORK CODE OF CONDUCT, WRITTEN BY AND FOR ALL Vunorri employees, designed to break down barriers, foster communication and encourage us to forget about our differences in job title, wealth, ability, and political beliefs. Let's remind ourselves: why would we want to forget about these intractable differences? Because forgiving and forgetting leads to understanding where our coworkers are coming from, and this allows us to work more effectively with each other. This understanding is the springboard from which Vunorri employees can jump forward in unison. We're doing this for ourselves, our families, and Vunorri Inc. It's high time we get to work, to cooperate with each other to make this business a better place to be, and to advance the cause of "us." It's time to give ourselves the chance to be happy again.

COMMITMENT CATEGORIES:

A.   Respect for the Work Process

B.   Respect for Each Other—Human Solidarity

C.   Respect for Business Goal No. 1—Happiness

A. RESPECT FOR THE WORK PROCESS

Let's care about doing great work, and let's create a workplace where it's easy to do so.

Employer Commitments to Employees

1. First and foremost, I will not ask my employees to do anything I would not be willing to do myself. And I will not create rules that I cannot follow myself. I realize that acting in such a manner destroys employee morale.

2. I will not publicly take credit for my employees' great ideas and hard work. This destroys employee morale even faster. I hired the talent here; there is my opportunity to take some credit.

3. I will give my employees direction. I want people with initiative (self-starters, as it were), but I do not want my employees to have to wonder what is most important to me.

4. I will provide my employees the tools and training they need to have a chance to succeed. I will mentor them, give them opportunities to advance when I can, and I will remember that it is not just the business owner who comes to work every day to achieve great things. Employees want to get better at what they do without having to leave our organization.

5. I will give my employees constructive feedback, taking both their career advancement and their feelings into consideration. Such feedback will be provided during the course of everyday business, or in an official performance review, or both. I will try to deliver feedback on projects and/or everyday job performance sooner rather than later, and I will do my best to deliver such commentary verbally. E-mails cannot always convey

exactly what I want to get across. And notes containing important feedback found on desks first thing in the morning constitute crappy communication. I don't want any employees to have to guess how they are doing. You have heard the management credo, "Hire good people and get out of their way." That sounds bold and adventurous, but I am not going to leave my employees out on an island. I am not here to slow anyone down with vulture-like micromanagement, but I will be here to both monitor and mentor.

6. I will try to provide some variety in my employees' work days. Working at Vunorri does not have to be like some Henry Ford assembly line. Cross-training would be helpful. I respect my employees' curiosity to know how things work, even in other departments.

7. I will listen to the ideas of my employees. It is almost embarrassing this has to be in The Agreement, but I promise to solicit employee feedback. Of course we cannot act upon every idea provided to us, but we know our employees are "on the front lines." Perhaps they are best suited to spot, troubleshoot and solve certain problems. I want my employees thinking creatively and critically. Please contribute to our most important discussions. I will listen. Surely, I do want buy-in from my employees, but what I really need is great ideas.

8. I will not be afraid to hire employees who are smarter than me. It is the sign of a great manager and a confident owner.

9. I will not keep dead weight around. I do not want to be mean and cutthroat, but I promise to build a workforce where our employees can excel, even if that means pulling the trigger on some tough decisions. One should not have to pick up the slack

for underperforming employees. That said, we are not going to make personnel decisions using Jack Welch-style stack rankings. Annually firing 10% of one's workforce is an apathetic, lackadaisical way to build a team.

10. I promise to take arguments between owners, or between owners and upper management, behind closed doors. Employees do not need to see or hear such things. Often, such strife can hurt employee morale, and can even make employees fear for their future. I need to keep that in mind.

11. I will remember that I may possess certain skillsets that my employees do not. Therefore, it may not be reasonable to expect from others sterling performance in areas where I excel. I will be patient. There was only one Michael Jordan on the Bulls.

12. I will keep in mind that my employees may not be as excited about the organization as I am. This is natural, as this business is my dream and not necessarily theirs.

Employee Commitments to Employer

13. I understand that my job is not a right, nor a privilege. The Legal department likes this one, which would normally give us pause. But it's a good prism to look through.

14. I will show up to work on time or will communicate when I can't. Cyborgs can't cover for me yet.

15. I promise to ignore my job description every once in a while. In other words, my employer will not hear the words "That's not my job" come out of my mouth.

16. I will never answer a question with "because that's the way it's always been done." That is a lazy, clown answer.

17. If I quit and give two weeks notice, I will not quit on Vunorri Inc. during those two weeks. Keep in mind: I am leaving for a reason and may be eagerly anticipating my last day, so it is possible my effort will not be 100%. But I will try. Maybe the HR department could even exit interview me and use my departing advice to help build a stronger organization going forward.

18. There is no need for me to be jealous of or compete with fellow employees. Quoting Simon Sinek, "When you compete with everyone else, no one wants to help you. When you compete against yourself, everyone wants to help you." People helping people. To quote Homer Simpson, that is "the glue that holds together the gears" of a team. A work culture with employees helping each other benefits everyone. I will work in concert with my coworkers. I will compete only with yesterday's self. My barometer is yesterday; I must be better today than I was the day before.

We Jointly Commit

19. As employees, we will challenge each other to be our very best. Doing great work gives human beings the sense of significance they need and desire.

20. Praise will be public; complaining and criticism (whether constructive or not) will be private.

21. We won't publicly present a problem without offering at least one viable solution. Chief Problem Identification Officer is not a staffed role at this organization.

22. When a fellow employee must work in complete concentration, I will try to give that employee a chance to work uninterrupted. What can wait...will wait.

23. We commit to not get caught up in each other's politics or religion. It has nothing to do with work (unless of course we found ourselves working for a political campaign, a politician or a religious organization). We need not be thinking or worrying about liberal or conservative, Catholic or Muslim. So, that means one cannot be talking politics and religion at work all the time. As individuals, we may have strong convictions, but work is not the place to be politically or religiously expressive. We are going to leave this stuff out of the office environment. And besides, people who cannot see past their own political and religious biases are like robots, and poorly programmed ones at that.

B. RESPECT FOR EACH OTHER— HUMAN SOLIDARITY

Let's care about each other. We may come from different tribes, backgrounds, and points of view, but we're all made from the same stuff.

Employer Commitments to Employees

24. Vunorri Inc. cannot always operate in a family-first manner, but we are going to try as hard as we can. The world is different now. Dads work in concert with moms to take care of their kids. Not everyone has a robust support network they can rely on. A sick child at home is a problem that a family needs to tend to. I will be as flexible as possible. An employee's family is going to be more important to them than our organization is, and I will work hard to remember that. We are not going to go out of business because an employee had to leave work to comfort a puking child. We should be stronger than that.

25. It may have been a long time since I was last a "blue collar" worker, or perhaps I have never been anything but "well off." This may cause me and my employees to think we do not have much in common, and in certain instances, this may be so. The entire point of this Agreement is to foster understanding by at least imagining what it is like to walk in each other's shoes, so I will try to do so if you, the employee, will try.

26. I will not discriminate in our hiring decisions, except when it comes to talent. I need great people, no matter what they look like. I will not base my choices on race, color, religion, creed, sex, national origin, age, disability, veteran status, or sexual orientation. In fact, to do so would be foolish, as I would be severely cutting down the available pool of talent from which to choose.

27. I have something extra to say about veterans. I will give veterans the same chance I give every job applicant. The fact that they "saw some crazy stuff" when serving their country in battle has nothing to do with anything. In fact, their ability to manipulate multi-million dollar equipment under extreme circumstances would seemingly make them very worthy candidates.

28. I will not ask prospective or current employees for their social media passwords, nor will I force them to show me what they've posted on their private social media accounts. This is a level of privacy invasion that is completely unacceptable. (Yes, this has happened)

29. Personality tests—sometimes referred to as "psychometric tests"—are stupid. They provoke anxiety and are rarely relevant to the position being offered. I may not yet be able to eliminate this stuff from the hiring process (old HR habits die

hard), and there may still be relevant uses for such testing, but I will not forget the alternative: sitting down and having a nice conversation with the employee or job applicant.

30. If an employee resigns, I will not make it hard on them. There is no need to haze or hate on people who are leaving the organization, even if they leave during a tough stretch. Timing is never good on things like this, and I acknowledge that. We need to look inward and see what happened, and we need to remember that these departing employees could turn out to be great walking, talking ambassadors for us (or just the opposite).

31. Letting people go from my employ is always awful. If I have to lay off or fire someone, I am going to try to follow some human guidelines. I will do it in person. I will do it one at a time and not in a group setting, Reverend Moon-style. I will do everything in my power not to lay off an employee in front of others. An employee will not initially receive this news via a letter, e-mail, or phone call. I will tell them to their face. I will talk with them in the morning; I won't have them work an entire day. I will not do it on a Friday (everybody's favorite work day, which shall not be ruined). I will also try to give the affected employee a soft landing. We will be careful and comforting in what we say, and if they want to come in after hours to grab their personal things, we will make that accommodation. Treating people in such a manner is the right thing to do. Each employee is some mom and dad's special little son or daughter.

32. With that in mind, do anything illegal at my business and your employment here will be over faster than a knife fight in a phone booth.

Employee Commitments to Employer

33. Times are changing. Whether we like it or not, the lines between our personal lives and our work lives are increasingly blurred. This can play to an organization's advantage, as each employee can now be a brand ambassador. I promise to remember that, as an employee, I represent the organization in almost everything I do. Whether with people in person or on social media, I will comport myself in a manner befitting Vunorri Inc. In other words, I will not scream profanities in a road rage tirade while wearing one of our company hats.

34. I recognize the need for my employer or manager to have rights, too. It is preposterous to think that, just because they are the ones in control, they do not have rights and needs. I realize it is hard to run an organization. The owners tend to work the most hours. I will not assume that their lives are a cakewalk.

35. I recognize the right of my employers to generate a profit. They have put capital at risk; any rewards are deserved. Being bitter about this is counterproductive. Whether their wealth was inherited or earned, there is nothing unfair about the disparity in our net worths. This should have nothing to do with my ability to perform my job at a high level.

36. I recognize and respect the unique skillset a CEO and upper management employees must possess. I understand competition is fierce for experienced, strong, well-connected leaders. Therefore, I will not begrudge them their compensation packages.

37. It is not Vunorri Inc.'s duty to create jobs. Mr. Vunorri started the organization to chase a dream, to solve a problem, to fill a hole in the market, and yes, to make money. The organization

does not exist to provide jobs. Jobs are a crucial and necessary byproduct of a great idea executed. They continue to exist because of sales, efficient operations, and people who take pride in their work.

We Jointly Commit

38. Above all, each Vunorri Inc. employee deserves to be treated with respect. Some employees are smarter, some work harder, some earn more, some make fewer mistakes, some have more challenging family lives, and some work better with others. All of these things being true, each employee deserves a heaping measure of respect. So, unless the words emanating from your mouth are "Great job!" or "I just made bacon," no yelling at coworkers. And no throwing stuff either.

39. I understand that Vunorri Inc. is made up of a diversity of people from different tribes, different socioeconomic backgrounds, different neighborhoods, different races, and different political parties. We are not always going to be best friends and we might not always agree on everything. In those circumstances, it is my job to try to get along with my coworkers, find solutions, and get the job done. I will try to work well with people of every race, color, religion, creed, sex, national origin, age, disability, veteran status, and sexual orientation. We have two things in common: we are all human, and we all work here. It might not seem like enough to build a trusting relationship on, but we're going to work to make it so.

40. We will remember that each employee at this organization, from the CEO to entry-level, is somebody's somebody. Each person is someone's precious little son or daughter. We treat

our own children with white-glove reverence. We will at least try a muted version of this with our fellow employees.

41. I will not take advantage of my fellow employee's good nature or soft side, should he or she have one.

42. We truly succeed when everyone profits. An unbalanced situation where either employer or employee holds an oversized advantage is simply not sustainable.

43. This Agreement is a work code of conduct, but is not a legally binding contract. Repeat, we agree that the words "The Happywork Agreement" will never be uttered in a court of law, ever, ever, *ever*! There are no legal consequences to receiving and reading The Happywork Agreement. During the inevitable employer-employee disagreements that will occur in the course of running the organization, if things do go awry, we will have only ourselves to answer to. The fear of that reckoning, and not of potential legal action based on the contents of this agreement, should be enough for us.

C.—RESPECT FOR BUSINESS GOAL NO. 1—HAPPINESS

Tactics, metrics, and margins are important. But, let's first focus on the most important foundational business goal: building a happy place to work. We need Vunorri Inc. to be a company where one can spend a happy, fulfilling 100,000 hours, and go home in a happy mood, ready to be a good spouse and parent.

We Jointly Commit

44. We have to find a way to work together in harmony. Not only is this the path to profit and prosperity, but perhaps more importantly, it is the path to a feeling of significance, which yields fulfillment, which yields happiness. It is OK to strive for happiness at work, and that is now Vunorri Inc.'s first business goal.

45. Money does not buy happiness (really, we haven't figured this out yet?). As a human being, there may be a limit to how much money I need, but there is no limit to the amount of fulfillment I want to experience. Money may be one person's barometer of success, but to quote Steve Jobs, "I'm here to put a dent in the universe."

46. And finally...

  • Ask your coworkers how they're doing. Smile while asking.

  • Surprise your cubicle-mate by getting her a coffee.

  • Don't leave those lunchroom dishes in the sink because everyone else has.

  • Stay late and help a colleague in need.

  • Ask a coworker if there's anything you can assist with.

  • Remember birthdays, especially if the employee is working that day.

  • Let the boss know when a coworker does a great job.

- Compliment a workmate on a job well done.

- Pass along a business lead when you can.

- Every once in a while, take the people who report to you to lunch.

- Offer to pick up lunch for busy coworkers who can't escape the office.

- Make the dish you're best at making and bring it to the office as a treat.

- If an employee's child is sick, send that parent home.

- Send sick employees home. Sick employees, stay home.

- Let an obviously hurried employee use the lunch-room microwave first.

- Hold the elevator or the door for someone.

- Allow employees to attend their kids' sporting events and recitals.

- Take up a collection during the holidays for a needy family.

- Cover for a sick employee so they don't return to a mountain of work.

- Hug someone who's down.

- Surprise your people once a year by sending them home early.

- Brew the coffee if no one else has handled it. That includes you, boss.

- Thank people when they do their job, even though it's their duty.

- Brandish a smile today.

- Stop talking for once and listen.

- Humility and empathy—try them on for size.

- Quite simply, be nice! And give. Give to others. This is what fills up your cup in life.

Never underestimate the power of a smile.

Never underestimate the power of unilateral kindness.

Never underestimate the power of human solidarity.

Received By (print name)

_____

(Are you now feeling differently toward your Vunorri coworkers? We really hope so.)

Employees initially read through The Happywork Agreement in near silence. After maybe five minutes, there were some whispers. After almost 10 minutes, some folks began speaking to each other in hushed tones. They inadvertently created small discussion groups of three, four, five employees—Vunorri associates discussing the Agreement's contents. Dick had told them 15 minutes, but after 20 minutes, the conversations were nearly boisterous, and he didn't want to interrupt them. Sam and Dick observed the room the entire time. Vunorri's employees weren't punching each other, which Sam and Dick took as a positive sign!

Finally, Dick asked the room to settle back down, and he again took the microphone. "Thanks everyone for taking the time to review The Happywork Agreement. Sam and I worked really hard on this, so we appreciate the attention you paid to it.

"We want everyone to take this initiative seriously. Come hell or high water, life is going to change around here. This is how we're going to conduct business at Vunorri going forward. All potential hires will know about this agreement. They will be told, 'This is the code we live by at Vunorri Inc. If this doesn't sit well with you, working here will prove to be a poor fit for you.' We're committed to operating in this way. This is a declaration of what we believe. HR will get on board with this.

"During the next few weeks, we're going to start sitting down in small groups and discussing the The Happywork Agreement's contents. Nothing's off the table—nothing! You'll all have a wide berth to speak your mind. And everyone is participating—employees *and* management. All employees will be included in these talks. Only through such conversations, even the uncomfortable and unpleasant ones, will we ever learn to respect each other. Only by talking to each other about the commitments in the Agreement can we learn to understand, respect, and accept Vunorri employees different than us.

"Some of the conversations will be thorny. I'd be worried if they *weren't*. Some awkward, difficult meetings, holding the promise of a new beginning for Vunorri, are certainly a preferred path to bickering, misery, and life malaise. We have to commit to this!"

Sam leaned in and whispered a reminder in Dick's ear.

"Oh, and I forgot. The Agreement you're holding in your hands is just a start. I think Sam and I have built a nice base here. During the next few weeks' meetings, we want to hear your thoughts. You have a voice in this. What's missing from the Agreement? What needs to go? What makes you uncomfortable? Let's collaborate to make The Happywork Agreement even better.

"Knuckling down with Sam on this document all weekend laid one fact bare: for my *entire* tenure as President, I've been asleep at the wheel. Well, I'm awake now, and I want to wake you guys up, too. I need to lead. That's what management does. That's what owners do. They lead. They don't whip.

"In summary, it's high time Vunorri Inc. becomes a kinder and happier place to work. It all boils down to this: if I treat you poorly, from where will you draw the strength to treat me any other way? That's it right there, guys. This place needs more nice.

"Now," he said, "I have one final question for you, 'cause some of you are looking at me kind of funny. I don't know if that's because I don't sound like myself, or if you're all in shock, or if you think this Agreement is just plain silly. You've had a chance to read it over, and you discussed it among yourselves a bit, too. So I'll ask you. I'll ask all of you: If we could get the majority of this Happywork Agreement to come true...if we could all adhere to most of the tenets of this Agreement, do you think this company would be a place you would want to work?"

Everyone thought about it, whispered thoughts to a neighbor, and looked at each other. Someone near the front raised a hand and said, "Mr. Vunorri, at first glance, it seems like a long road to travel, to be honest with you. But yes, if we all lived by this Agreement, Vunorri would be a much happier place to work."

Rod unexpectedly took a few steps forward, until he was standing near Dick at the front of the warehouse. He peered over his shoulder to scan the crowd of Vunorri faithful, and then loudly proclaimed, "I think we're in."

Dick said, "Well OK, that's all any of us should need to hear. Let's get to work and make it happen."

CHAPTER 17

REDEMPTION + SALVATION

As SHOCKING AS IT MAY SEEM, SITTING AT THE COFFEE SHOP was getting old.

Three weeks had passed since the big breakthrough at Vunorri, the subsequent two weeks of Happywork Agreement meetings and the end of the engagement. Sam had been getting out of the house in the mornings, drinking mug after mug of coffee, updating his website. Surely a Vunorri case study would generate some inbound leads, and he needed some leads. Spending five solid, intense weeks at Vunorri had him off the sales beat. He was going to need to land a project soon.

On top of that, he was facing an acute case of "Consultant Emptiness and Loneliness." A major letdown. He brought a ton of value to Vunorri. This was, by all accounts, his best work by far. Drawing on his experience, and with Charlie's sage advice, he had transformed their culture. Harvard case study material. He simultaneously convinced a well-off CEO to see the error of his ways and consider life from the viewpoint of his employees, and he helped the employees learn to respect management. *And* he caught a crook, saving the company! He even drafted the plan that placated the bank. But, like always, he didn't get to stick around for the party. Everyone else at

Vunorri got to reap the benefits of what they had sown—to work toward their larger and now-shared purpose, and to build upon their successes and make a long-term difference. Sam, on the other hand, was looking for his next meal.

While doing important "thinking work" like writing case studies, Sam was never smart enough to disconnect from electronic distractions like e-mail and social media. Perhaps a good thing, because he received an e-mail that made his heart skip a beat.

It was from Dick Vunorri. He wanted Sam to stop by and say hi.

"Hi, Sam, how are you!??" Dick bellowed with a huge grin on his face. "Happy Friday! We've missed you! How are things?"

"Not bad. I've been enjoying some family time, working on my website, and recovering. How's business around here?"

"Oh Sam, *much better. So* much better. Of course things aren't perfect. Some old grudges remain, and they'll take time to die off. Not everyone agrees with every tenet of The Happywork Agreement, but our disagreements are now respectful—we talk to each other! As you know, I immediately fired Melinda, and a few others have quit. Probably for the best. Superimposing the Agreement on top of our workplace weeded out many of the troublemakers. Neil's obviously gone, and in all sorts of trouble. But the people who remained...they're working together in ways I would've never expected. *We're getting along.* More excitement, more smiles. People seem to *want* to come to work. Crazy! We still have a long way to go, but I'm shocked at how much happier everyone is. With The Happywork Agreement's help, we're changing our workplace."

Sam was pleased that his work had borne fruit. Dick really seemed like a changed man.

"Plus," Dick said, "our forensic accountants found nearly a million dollars in phony invoices Neil paid to himself over the past few years. Insurance is going to reimburse us. We're not completely out of the financial woods, but I'll be able to make a substantial payment to the bank. I'm confident we'll be completely out of debt in a year or two. I can't thank you enough for that, Sam."

Sam beamed with pride. "I'm just glad we found it in time. What did you do about Neil's position?"

"I promoted Josie. She's way sharper than anyone even knew. So much was new to her because Neil kept his knowledge close to the vest, but she's jumped in head first. She's young, but smart as a whip.

"People miss you around here, Sam! Folks ask about you almost every day. I wish you had stopped by sooner."

"Sorry about that, Dick," Sam said. "I've been doing a little marketing, looking for my next gig."

Dick looked at Sam with a sly grin. Very sly.

"Sam, I called you in for a reason. Like I said, we're doing well here. So much better! We've all got the warm fuzzies now, you know? But we still have a long road ahead of us—a tremendous amount of work. I'm gonna need people to stick together and work as a team as we try to fix these problems. We're trying to live The Happywork Agreement, and I'm doing my best to play the role, but I'm pulled in so many directions. We can't go back to the way things were. We need an anchor, someone to keep us honest and on the right track. This was really all your doing. I have a job for you here. I need you to come back, Sam. I need you to help us live this out."

Sam stared at Dick, in shock. Was he hearing what he thought he was hearing? He practically forgot to blink as he sat there, astonished. Until...the corners of his mouth broke down and uncontrollably created the warmest grin.

"Sam, I'd like you to be my Chief Operations Officer, second in command. You'll have your hands in every department, much like you did during those five weeks."

"Dick, that's...this is...*wow*!" Sam exclaimed. He wanted to blurt out *yes*, but he also knew that sleeping on it, due diligence, talking it over with his wife, not making a snap decision blah blah blah whatever. He *wanted* this. He realized he'd be coming into a challenging situation, but he had done that with the five-week consulting engagement—what could have been more challenging than the old Vunorri Inc.?—and had passed with flying colors. The contributions he made at Vunorri felt so gratifying, so satisfying, and now he would get a chance to build upon them. He was going to be able to live a work life of significance. It was a situation where, as Dick admitted, everyone wasn't yet completely happy, but now it had such promise. He was appropriately nervous, but knew he was making a good decision.

"Well, Sam, whaddaya think?"

Sam did not hesitate. "You bet. I'm in."

"*Awwww* Sam, that's *great*! People are gonna be so happy about this!"

"Well, I...I missed you guys too," Sam said sheepishly. His emotions were knocking him a bit off balance. Still, they were emotions to savor.

"Let's talk compensation," Dick said. "For a senior management position like this, I'm thinking..."

Sam raised his right hand to stop Dick in his tracks. "Dick, it's not about the money. It's about the chase. It's about who I can help. It's about caring for others when they need it most. Like Steve Jobs said, it's about making a dent in the universe. I'll come in first thing Monday morning and we'll hammer out the details. We'll make it work. Sound good?"

"You got it. Welcome to the team!"

Sam swelled with pride. It wasn't about the paycheck, and it never would be. This was about enjoying life to the fullest, even those 100,000 hours of work. This was about creating happiness from sadness. To put it plainly, Sam would no longer destroy people's lives in order to solve a business equation and print money. He wanted to build things, and feel the warm embrace of contentment. He had gone through the ringer at Vunorri and moved a mountain. He had changed people's lives, and it felt *good*. And over five weeks, he had changed, too. The road ahead was a work life worth living.

"See you on Monday, Sam."

"Thanks so much, Dick. I can't wait." A wave of gratitude for a new old friend suddenly swept over him. "Wow. I owe Charlie so much," Sam mused aloud.

"Come again?" Dick quipped with a confused look on his face.

"You know, Charlie! Older white guy, wears short-sleeve dress shirts, works in your mailroom..."

"You mean my dad's been here?"

-THE END-

ACKNOWLEDGMENTS

I AM FASCINATED WITH AND OFTEN THINK ABOUT HOW PEOPLE step into roles that they hadn't previously played. For instance, what was it like to be Brad Pitt before he was famous, or more to the point, how much different is his life now? Or, to choose some contemporaries to whom I can aspire, what was it like to be Seth Godin or Malcolm Gladwell or Chris Brogan before they wrote something that everyone just loved? And what was "the jump" like for them? Was there one special person who lent them a hand? Were there seminal moments they'll never forget? I've always been interested in how a person makes that jump, the steps along the way, the literal machinations of making the move from the person that people thought they were to the person people think they are now, and their lives thereafter.

Here, I am thanking the people who helped me take a whole bunch of different steps along the way. I was knee-deep in a 20-year career in accounting that I wasn't meant for. I was an accountant, until I wasn't anymore. I became a social media strategist who people often called an expert, a guru, even a "Social Media Yoda" (embarrassing! But kinda funny). People tell me they find this career change of mine fascinating and amazing, and they really seem to mean it when they say it, so I believe them.

While the career change doesn't amaze me anymore, the existence of this book does. It's a huge step toward something I truly care about—changing the way we treat each other. Sometimes, I simply cannot believe that this book is alive and in your hands. Do you understand what I mean to say here? I was scared, didn't think I could do it, and thought I'd never get this book published. *I thought I would fail*, like I had failed before at this job or that test.

I didn't believe in myself, but here we are! How did this happen? How??? The only reason I can think of is that I have a team of friends who inexplicably believed in me, and a group of authors I learned from. What would I do without you? You deserve all the thanks in the world. Consider this to be a big thank-you hug to all of you.

First, to my wife Julie—The creation of this book was an effort that you had to endure. Frankly, you've had to endure much more than just this book. But you should know that you helped me make a dream of mine come true. Thank you for reading and critiquing my writing, and thank you for supporting me the whole way. I'm a fool without you.

To my mom and dad—I was a rotten child. Thanks for tolerating and surviving my upbringing.

Susan Baroncini-Moe—if it wasn't for you, this book isn't published by Sound Wisdom. You helped me find my new home. That's so amazing! Gracias!

To my friends at Sound Wisdom—David Wildasin, Nathan Martin, John Martin, and Christina Lynch. You guys are the best. When other publishers curtly said, "No," you were there for two-hour conference calls. You cared about the quality of this book. Your advice and stewardship was key. And John, you convinced me the Oxford Comma wasn't pure literary evil.

Peter Shankman—your book *Nice Companies Finish First* was helpful. But it's your friendship that matters to me. I mean, maybe "friendship" isn't the right word since we've, to date, only hung out in person once. But the term "friendship" has been completely redefined by the Internet. I'll say this—"Famous people" don't really realize what they mean to their fans. Just knowing you, Peter, and you knowing me in the small way that you do, gave me such a boost. It made me believe, when my Seth Godin "lizard brain" wanted to shut down because it had crushing doubts. My relationship with you made me believe I could pull this off.

John Morgan—you're an inspiration to me, too. You answered all of my dumb questions about writing and public speaking. A kind word from you always picks me up. It's good to have friends like you. Your encouragement means so much to me.

Mark Schaefer—thank you for that all-important conversation we had on February 2, 2013. After talking with you, the wind was at my back.

Bob Burg—what would the world do without you? I consider you our modern day Dale Carnegie. You wrote the first-ever, and only business book that ever made me cry—*The Go-Giver*. Embarrassing to admit, but true. I had not planned on writing a business parable like you. My book was going to be a nonfiction look at happiness in the workplace. Besides encouragement from my publisher, I saw you use a parable to make the points you wanted to make, and you did it so well—twice! I wasn't sure I would be able to pull it off, but you inspired me. Thank you for that.

To David Siteman Garland—without you, there is no Reimer book. I met you for coffee on January 19, 2010 (a full five years before this book saw the light of day) and you asked me, "Why are you waiting to share your knowledge with the world?" (I hadn't yet started blogging or doing speaking engagements.) I said I felt like I had to accomplish something with Rizzo Tees first before anyone would listen, and you told me that was dead wrong. You said, "Start sharing now. You know stuff, start sharing it." You gave me confidence to talk about what I believed via Twitter, Facebook, and my blog(s), and the advice changed my life. It's funny to consider how that morning might have been a throwaway moment in your life, while it was a pivot point in mine. For all of us, it goes to show that you never know how much *your* helping hand will mean to someone else.

Seth Godin—I did it! I shipped my creativity! It might not be much, but it's my symphony, my work of art, and I'm glad it escaped my brain. You said the world needs us and our art, and I just went ahead and believed you. Reading *Linchpin* during a crucial part of this book's development process was a turning point for me.

To Chris Brogan—as I was learning my way in this new social world, trying to escape the world of accounting, I read your blog every day. You were one of my teachers, a giver. Your prolific blog posting was one of the first examples I can identify in my life of what I'd call an "unbalanced equation" (my parents were probably the very first). All you did was give, and all I did was take. You wrote and wrote, and I read and read. The knowledge I gained helped me blaze a new trail.

Gary Vaynerchuk—what can I say, dude? I know you'll never read this 'cause you don't read books, but you've meant so much to my life. Your Web 2.0 talk shook something loose in me. What was it you said? "Stop doing 'stuff' you hate!" I heard that message during a tough time in my work life and thought, "I have to make a change." I can't bother to care how tired this word sounds—Gary, you *inspired* me.

To Sharon Rohrbach—thank you for believing in me, and for working so hard to protect the most vulnerable in our world.

To my attorney, Jeff Schultz—quoting Biggie Smalls, "Don't you know bad boys move in silence and violence." That's you, without the violence, of course. We'll leave it at that.

Jim Harper—you started reading my chicken scratch a day or two before the death of your Boxing Clever partner, Mike Borman. Such a terrible time in your life. Anyway, working on my life's most important work, as your friend was taken from you...it was a tough time for you, and poignant for me. Your positive feedback (words like "scary talented" and "revolutionary idea") gave me the big head I needed to ship this art. I shall never forget July 2013 and the help you provided me.

Simon Sinek's book *Start with Why* tweaked my understanding of storytelling, and changed everything for me. Simon, I met you in St. Louis in May 2013 and was blown away by your warmth and engaging personality. You gave me a special Golden Circle coin, asking me to join your movement. Consider it joined. (I had the coin tested; it was NOT real gold.)

Olivier Blanchard—you don't suffer fools lightly. You keep me on my toes, and I appreciate your offers of help to me. So kind of you. I consider myself a pea in your pod.

Phil Gerbyshak—on July 29, 2012, you had a serious multi-hour discussion with me at Alterra Coffee in Milwaukee that gave me so many new perspectives to think about.

To my trusty proofreaders—Jenn Cloud, Greg Bussmann, Eliot Frick, Dave Gray (who was especially tough on me), Mary Steinau, my mom, and my wife. And thanks to Arlene Maminta Browne, Clay Hebert, Brad Hogenmiller, Emily Pirraglia Knippa, Travis Sheridan,

Mike Spakowski, Jeremy Nulik, Paul Crane, Peter Strople, and Sam Silverstein for the advice and encouragement along the way.

To Steve Hartman, my cover designer—thanks for putting up with me. And to Cat McMillan for helping me with my book proposal.

To Bill Sawalich, for taking the photo of me on the About the Author page, one in which I look presentable.

To Frank Hemmekam—thank you for creating the wonderful and free font "Baron" used on the front cover for the title.

For helping me during research, I must thank John Hilliard, Matt Ridings, Ryan Farmer, Tabitha Tomko, Greg Bussmann, and too many friends on Facebook.

To people I care about: my brother Mat Reimer, Jon Falk, Mike De Vlieger, Jeff Mertz, Julio Varela, Richard Callow, Troika Brodsky, Zach Hickert, Joe Sorge, Mike Tomko, Chris Krehmeyer, Eammon Azizi, Angela Hutti, Mark Reardon, and everyone else I forgot to mention who lent me a hand along the way.

To my heroes—Nelson Mandela, Martin Luther King Jr., Rosa Parks, Christopher Hitchens, Sam Harris, Morrissey, Dale Carnegie, Bertrand Russell, my Mom and Dad, my Grandpa Walter Reimer, and my grandma Ann Reimer.

I've forgotten several important people. By definition, I don't know who you are. It will eventually come to me. I'm sorry I omitted your name here. You have my most sincere thanks.

Finally, you should read these books: anything by Bob Burg but especially *The Go-Giver* (co-authored by John David Mann), Dale Carnegie's *How to Win Friends and Influence People*, Peter Shankman's *Nice Companies Finish First*, Gary Vaynerchuk's *The Thank You Economy*, Matt Haig's *The Humans*, Tim Ferriss' *The 4-Hour Workweek*, Dan Pink's *Drive*, Richard Sheridan's *Joy, Inc.*,

John Morgan's *Brand Against The Machine*, David Meerman Scott's *The New Rules of Marketing and PR*, Bertrand Russell's *Human Knowledge: Its Scope and Limits*, Jason Fried and David Heinemeier Hansson's *Rework*, Chris Brogan and Julien Smith's *Trust Agents*, Dave Gray's *The Connected Company*, Simon Sinek's *Start With Why*, John Jantsch's *The Commitment Engine*, and Seth Godin's *Linchpin*. These works of art are self-education at its finest.

THREE INVITATIONS:

1. To discuss this book with friends and sympathetic strangers on Twitter, Facebook, and Instagram, use the hashtag #Happywork.

2. So many of us have had traumatic work experiences similar to the ones you read about in this book. I'd love to hear from you. What work battles have you fought? If you're feeling up to it, please share your stressful, awful stories with me at Happywork@ChrisReimer.com. Sometimes it helps to just talk about it.

3. To book me to speak about topics covered in this book, message me at Happywork@ChrisReimer.com

ABOUT THE AUTHOR

Chris Reimer is an award-winning communications strategist, a humanist, and a student of human interaction. He founded *Rizzo Tees*, a t-shirt company headquartered in his basement. He went on to become possibly the only human alive who went from being a CPA and CFO to a marketing and communications strategist. He is a guest lecturer at Washington University and resides in St. Louis, MO with his wife and two daughters. Join him on HappyworkBook.com or say hi on Twitter at @ChrisReimer (99% chance he'll say hi back).